THE MOUTH OF
THE NIGHT

THE MOUTH OF
THE NIGHT

❧❀❧

Gaelic Stories Retold by
IRIS MACFARLANE

Illustrated by John Lawrence

MACMILLAN PUBLISHING CO., INC.
NEW YORK

Macmillan Publishing Co., Inc., 866 Third Avenue, New York, N.Y. 10022
First American edition, 1976
Printed in the United States of America

1 2 3 4 5 6 7 8 9 10

Library of Congress Cataloging in Publication Data

Macfarlane, Iris.
    The mouth of the night.

    A selection of re-translated stories first published in Tales of the West Highlands by J. F. Campbell.
    CONTENTS: The sea maiden.—The Sporran full of gold.—The old gray man of spring.—How the Great Turisgale met his death. [etc.]
    1. Tales, Celtic. [1. Folklore, Celtic]   I. Lawrence, John, date II. Campbell, John Francis, 1822–1885. Tales of the West Highlands. III. Title.
PZ8.1.M166Mo4   398.2'09411   75–31576   ISBN 0–02–765430–3

CONTENTS

INTRODUCTION   1

THE SEA MAIDEN   6

THE SPORRAN FULL OF GOLD   22

THE OLD GRAY MAN OF SPRING   31

HOW THE GREAT TURISGALE MET HIS DEATH   38

THE BLUE FALCON   46

THE WIZARD'S GILLIE   57

THE THREE SHIRTS OF CANNACH COTTON   65

THE SHARP GRAY SHEEP   77

THE SON OF THE KING OF THE CITY OF STRAW   82

THE SHIP THAT SAILED ON SEA AND LAND   95

THE BROWN BEAR OF THE GREEN GLEN   102

BLACKBERRIES IN FEBRUARY   112

THE MAN WHO COULDN'T GET MARRIED   123

THE KNIGHT OF THE RED SHIELD   131

Gu mo charaid
MAIRI NIC GILL-EATHAIN,
bardess of Black Point, Grimsay,
the warmth of whose smile and peats,
and the help given with her beautiful, difficult language,
largely made this book possible.

THE MOUTH OF
THE NIGHT

INTRODUCTION

"There was a king and a knight, as there was and will be, as grows the fir tree, some of it crooked and some of it straight. . . ." So begins one of the old stories, the *sgeulachdan*, told through the long winter evenings in the Highlands and Islands of Scotland; and the words bring the authentic shiver down the spine, half pleasure, half fear, of entering a world both magical and mysterious, and yet in some way familiar.

There are still old people in the Hebrides who remember the evenings round the peat fire, the men sitting in a row on the long wooden bench, passing the tobacco pipe and making the netting for their creels; the women spinning, and the stories teased out like the wool, and wound up again round the wheel of memory until the ends were all tied up and tucked away. Life was very hard in those days, but one of its compensations was the neighborliness of those story-telling nights, with the sea wind swirling past the rounded corners of the stone houses, hardly rattling the deep windows, houses that harbored, as well as family and friends, cattle and horses and poultry under their thatch and turf roofs.

That was fifty years ago, but a hundred and twenty years ago, when J. F. Campbell walked round the islands, a knapsack on his back, collecting the stories of which the fourteen in this volume are but a small selection, the community he entered was as untouched as any in the world. Many of the islanders could speak nothing but the Gaelic, the majority could not read, so

1

that the feats of memory by which they told night-long stories, without pause or hesitation or repetition, were really remarkable. The fact that the stories had been handed down by word of mouth, generation after generation, gave them a special importance. This was the original, the archetypal material, from which Grimm and Hans Andersen, the Norse and Icelandic sagas, and even, elusively but quite definitely, the Arabian Nights and the Panchatantra, were drawn. The comparisons are obvious, but each people have imprinted on the stuff of the stories, in colors of their choosing, the character and shape of their own lives.

Campbell describes a house in which he sat to hear some of the stories, a house at the ford joining South Uist to Benbecula, a place I know well. "The house is built of a double wall of loose boulders, with a layer of peat three feet thick between the walls. The ends are round and the roof rests on the inner wall, leaving room for a crop of yellow gowans. A man might walk around the roof on the top of the wall. There is but one room with two low doors, one on each side of the house. The fire is on the floor; the chimney is a hole above it and the rafters are hung with pendants and festoons of shining black reek. . . . They support a covering of turf and straw, and stones and heather ropes, which keep out the rain well enough."

The little old houses are being abandoned, sadly, for they are prettier than the modern bungalows that replace them, but much harder to live in in many ways too—dark, and damp, and with a constant need to be rethatched. But the people who live in the new bungalows haven't changed at all. "A small, active, intelligent race, with dark hair and eyelashes, and gray eyes, quick, clever and pugnacious," is how Campbell describes them. They seem to me gentle rather than pugnacious, perhaps because at last they are freeing themselves from the stranglehold of landlord and factor, but the rest of this description I would agree with entirely: "I have wandered amongst the peasantry of many countries and this trip but confirmed my impression. There are few peasants that I think so highly of, none that I like so well." He goes on to sum them up. They have, he says, "the delicate natural tact which discovers, and the good taste which avoids, all that would hurt or offend a guest. . . . I have never found a boor or a churl in a Highland bothy." Exchanging the word peasant for islander, bothy for bungalow, the words are the best I know to describe the people of the Outer Hebrides.

It was from these people that Campbell and his collectors took down the stories in the Gaelic and translated them word for word as nearly as they could—rightly, for this was precious stuff. The result was published in his famous collection, *Tales of the West Highlands,* a book which is a treasure trove for the folklorist, but one which a child would find difficulty in reading. So much of the original story was "acted" when orally recited that in places the text becomes almost too contracted to follow; much of it too was fierce and vengeful, recalling a time of battle and blood feud, and as such not suitable for children. This is my excuse for retranslating the stories, trying to alter as little as possible, but of necessity softening, and sorting and linking. Something is lost, something is always lost, but I hope that the stories will now reach children who would—at an even greater loss to themselves—have missed them.

Words are strange things—they not only speak for themselves, they set up echoes in the mind. When you change from one language to another you lose the original impact of sound, and the echo is a different one. "Scrithean," gravel or small stones in Gaelic, is exactly the sound of pebbles washed down

3

by the tide, soft and gritty; "tonn," a wave, falls with the liquid weight of water; "sligean," shells, clatter and hiss; "latha na latha" is "on a day of days" and yet it isn't, because "latha" as pronounced in the Gaelic is a soft and seductive word, unlike the more prosaic "day." More especially the rhythm changes in translation, and since the secret of all good writing, both poetry and prose, is in the rhythm, it is impossible to retain either impact or echo or pace.

But I hope something of the original has come through, and something of the lost world of which the stories speak; a world of singing apples and healing wells and birds who are soothsayers; where rushes hide magic cauldrons and water bulls, and if you sit behind green hillocks, "behind the wind and before the sun," you may be sure to see a blue filly before too long; where blessings and curses follow you like sun and shadow, and on the edge of the sea, floating at the brown rim of the world, is the Green Isle which haunts the imagination of every islander.

I have seen islands floating; here in the Hebrides I have reencountered a world I left in childhood. It may be the quality of the light, or the silence, or their uncommitted air, offering neither fuss nor prettiness, that give to the Western Isles their peculiar glamour; glamour in its original sense, to cast a spell, to fascinate the eyes so that they see what is not. In the white mornings, or at the mouth of the night when the small brown birds are going to their nests—not in walnut trees but in banks and walls—and the blue peat smoke rises from the chimneys, and the track of the duck leads to the sea's edge where the boats are pulled up seven lengths on the grass where no wind can blacken them and no sun burn; then one can almost see the shadow of the giant fall across the hill, or the three heads of the Uile-Beast rise from the loch.

INTRODUCTION

Vulnerable as we all are, at the mercy of the next deep-sea oil driller which will chase away every Beast and pollute every well of green water between the Hebrides and Greenland, it is important I think to try and preserve the innocent and ritual world of the *sgeulachdan*, in our minds and in the minds of our children. For all its wicked stepmothers and scheming hen-wives it was essentially a world where there were remedies and choices, where things came right after exactly appropriate actions. We can never be too grateful to Campbell of Islay for rediscovering this world for us.

THE SEA MAIDEN

There was, before this, a poor old fisherman, and one year he caught little fish. On a day of days, and he fishing, a sea maiden rose up beside his boat and asked if he was catching fish. He said that he was not.

"What reward would you give me if I sent you plenty of fish?" said the sea maiden.

"Ah," said the old man, "I have not much to give."

"Will you give me your first son?"

"I would, but I have no son. There will never be a son of mine, for my wife and I are old."

"Tell me everything you have," said the sea maiden.

"I have only an old mare, and an old dog; these, with my wife, are all I have in the great world."

"Well then," said the sea maiden, "here are three grains to give to your wife tonight, and three to give to your dog, and three to your horse. Another three you must plant behind your house. In time your wife will have three sons, and your dog three puppies, and your mare three foals, and three identical trees will grow behind your house. When a son of yours shall die, so will a tree of yours wither. Now, go home, and meet me again when your son is three years of age. You will catch plenty of fish after this."

Everything happened as the sea maiden said, and the old man caught plenty of fish. But as the three years drew to an end he became mournful and heavy-hearted.

6

Each day, as it came, brought the day of his meeting with the sea maiden closer behind it; and on that day he went fishing as usual, but he did not take his son with him.

The sea maiden rose by the side of the boat, and asked:

"Did you bring your son to me?"

"Ah, fancy," exclaimed the old man. "I did not bring him, for I forgot that this was the day."

"Well, you may have another four years of him," said the sea maiden, "to see if it will be easier to part from him then." She lifted a beautiful, big baby from under the sea. "Is your son as fine as this?" she laughed.

The old man went home full of comfort and consolation because he would have another four years of his son, and he went on catching plenty of fish. But at the end of the four years sorrow struck and filled him, and he could neither take his food nor do his work. His wife could not understand what had come over him. The old man did not know what to do, but he knew that as before he would not take his son with him when he went fishing.

On the day of their third meeting, the sea maiden rose from the side of the boat, and asked:

"Did you bring your son to me?"

"Ah, fancy, I forgot him again," said the old man.

"Go home then," said the sea maiden, "and at the end of seven years, be sure to remember. It will not be any easier for you to part with him, but you will catch plenty of fish as usual."

The old man went home full of joy; he had another seven years of his son, and before the seven years were past he himself would be dead, and would see the sea maiden no more. Heigh ho for his hopes!

The seven years passed, and the old man was still there, and grew troubled once more. He hardly knew whether it was day or night, and his eldest son asked him what it was that was troubling him.

The old man said his trouble could not be shared, it belonged to him and nobody else, but his son told him he must know. So in the end the old man described his meetings with the sea maiden, and the promise he had made to her.

"Do not be troubled on my account," said his son. "I will never oppose you."

"You shall not go to the sea maiden, you shall not," cried his father, "even if I never catch another fish."

"If you will not allow me to go with you," said his son, "go instead to the smithy, and let the smith make me a great, strong sword, and I will go and seek my fortune at the ends of the earth."

So the old man went to the smithy, and the smith made a sword, but when his son shook it twice in the air, it splintered into a hundred pieces. He told his father to get him a sword twice as heavy, but when it was made and brought to him the first shake broke it in two. A third time the smith made a sword, and this was the heaviest and strongest he had ever fashioned, and the fist must be powerful, said the smith, even to hold it.

The old man took the sword to his son, and he shook it once or twice.

"It will do," he said. "Now it is time to go on my journey."

In the morning he put a saddle on the black horse, son of the old gray mare, and with his black dog by his side went out to ride the world, and make the earth his pillow. After he had ridden for a short while, he came across the carcass of a sheep lying by the side of the road. Near the carcass were a great fox, a hawk, and an otter, wondering how to divide the sheep, indeed how to break it up at all.

He dismounted and with his sword divided the meat between the three, two shares to the fox, one share to the hawk and the otter.

"For this," said the great fox, "if swiftness of foot or sharpness of teeth can ever help you, remember me, and I will come to you."

"For this," said the otter, "if water-webbed legs at the bottom of a pool can help you, remember me and I will come to you."

"For this," said the hawk, "if power of wing or bent talon can help you, remember me and I will come to you."

He thanked them and rode on his way, and after a while he reached the king's palace. There he found work as a herdsman, and as much milk as he drew from the herd, so much would be his pay. The first day he drove his charges out, but the grazings were bare, and he got little milk from them that evening, so there was little barley bread for him to eat.

Next day he drove the cattle farther, right into the mountains, and came to a green glen with grass richer than he had ever seen before. All day the cows grazed contentedly, and he with equal content watched them, but in the evening as he was rounding them up to take them home, a huge shadow fell on the grass of the glen.

"Ho, haw, hograck," roared a great voice, and out from the mountains stepped a giant, his sword in his hand. "My teeth have grown rusty from famine for your flesh," he thundered. "Those cattle are mine for this is my land, and you are a dead man."

"Take them if you can," said the herdsman. "It may be easier to say than to do."

With a great clash of sword blades they came to grips, and the herdsman knew that he was far from his friends, with only his enemy close to him. His life was in his own hands. His great clean-bladed sword drew sparks of fire from the giant's sword; and in the clang and the flash of battle the black dog leapt at the giant's throat, and in that instant the herdsman swept off his head.

Then he leapt on his black horse and went off to look for the giant's house, and before long, behind a rocky spur he found it. In his hurry to leave, the giant had left all the gates open, and inside was such pomp, such heaps of gold and silver, such profusion of silks and velvets and laces! The herdsman and his dog and his horse stared at it in wonder, but without taking anything they turned and drove the herd home.

At the mouth of the night they reached the king's palace, and the cows gave plenty of milk that night, and there was plenty of barley bread, with curds and treacle. The king was delighted to have found a man so skilled, and for some weeks the herdsman continued to take his cattle to the green glen in the mountains; but at last it grew bare, and he decided he must drive them farther to look for new pasture.

He had not ridden far when he came to a great park, full of rich grass, and here he loosed his cattle, but they had hardly begun to crop the grass when another huge shadow fell across the meadow. Behind the shadow was another giant, wild, fiery, and enraged.

"Ho, haw, hograck," roared the giant. "Only a drink of your blood will quench my thirst this night. This is my land, and you are a dead man."

"We will see about that," said the herdsman. "It may be easier said than done."

With a flash and clatter of blades they came to grips, and it seemed as if the giant must overcome the herdsman, but as he

10

gasped for breath he called for his dog, and with one leap the dog was at the giant's throat, and with one sweep of the herdsman's sword the giant's head was off. He dragged himself and his cattle home exhausted that night, but what milk there was for the king's house, and how delighted the king was with his herdsman!

For a time he continued to take his cattle to the green park, but one evening instead of the happy greeting the dairymaids usually gave him, he was met with tears and lamentation. He asked why they wept on this beautiful evening, and they replied that there was a great beast in the loch, with three heads, who claimed a victim every year. This year the lot had fallen on the king's daughter.

"And at midday tomorrow she is to meet the Beast at the head of the loch, and her strong suitor is going to try to rescue her," said the milkmaids.

"What suitor is that?" asked the herdsman.

"Oh, he is a great general," said the milkmaids, "and if he kills the Beast, he will marry the king's daughter, for the king has said that whoever rescues his daughter will get her in marriage."

In the morning, as midday approached, the king's daughter and her hero went to the black corrie at the head of the loch, and almost at once the Beast rose from the middle of the water. No sooner did the general see the three horrible heads than he took fright and slunk off to hide, and the king's daughter trembled with the thought that there was nobody to rescue her. She looked wildly around, and there riding down the loch-side was a handsome young man on a black horse, with a black dog by his side. He was fully armed, his armor glittering in the sun, his dog gleaming blacker than the water beside him.

"There is gloom on your face, oh maiden," said the young man. "What are you doing here?"

"What does it matter?" said the king's daughter. "I shall not be here long."

"Do not speak like that," said the young man. "I will not believe it."

"It's not long since a hero as strong as you retreated," she said.

"Only a true hero is fit for this fight," he answered.

He dismounted from his horse, and lay down on the bank beside her, telling her to wake him, if he fell asleep, as soon as the Beast approached the bank.

"What is waking for you?" she asked.

"Waking for me is for that ring of yours to be put on my little finger," he replied.

He had not slept long, when the king's daughter saw the Beast approach the bank of the loch. She took the ring from her finger and put it on that of the young man beside her, and at once he leapt up. With his sword in his hand and his dog at his side he ran to the water's edge, and then there was a great slupertash-slapertash as he and the Beast plunged and struck and lashed. The black dog leapt at the writhing body of the Beast, and on the bank the king's daughter trembled with terror, as first one and then the other disappeared beneath the raging water.

At last with a mighty effort he struck one of the heads from the Beast, and one great roar came from it which echoed from

the crags, and flecks of foam like snow whirled from the churned water from one end of the loch to the other; and then in a blink the monster was gone.

"Good luck and success such as this follow you wherever you go, young man," said the king's daughter. "For myself, I will be safe for one night. Then the Beast will come back, and keep coming, until his last two heads are taken from him."

The young man put a rope through the head of the Beast, and gave it to the king's daughter, telling her to bring it with her to the loch next day. The he went back to his cows, and she set off for the palace with the Beast's head on her shoulders. She had not gone far when out of the bushes slunk the general, her suitor, and he told her he would kill her if she did not say that it was he who cut off the head.

"Oh, I will say it," said the king's daughter. "What other hero but you could have fought with the Beast?"

When they got back to the palace, the head was on the shoulders of the general, and its blood was on his hands. There was great rejoicing that the king's daughter had returned alive and well, and next morning when the two of them set off together, there was no doubt that such a hero would deliver her from the Beast again. But when they reached the loch, and the dreadful form of the monster stirred the water, the general fled as he had done the day before. And almost at once appeared the rider on the black horse, whom the king's daughter knew at once, though his dress had changed.

"Indeed, I am happy to see you," she said. "I hope you will handle your sword as you did yesterday. Dismount and take deep breaths in readiness."

Even as she spoke they saw steam rising from the middle of the loch, the fiery breath of the Uile-Beast. But the young man lay down by the side of the king's daughter and said:

14

"If I should sleep before the Beast comes to the side of the loch, waken me."

"What is waking for you?" asked she.

"Waking for me is to take the earring you wear, and put it in my ear," he said.

He had hardly closed his eyes when the king's daughter cried, "Wake, wake!" But he did not stir, so she took the ring from her ear, and put it in his, and at once he leapt up and ran to the water's edge to meet the Beast. Then there was a great slupertash-slapertash, and neighing and braying, and they fought for many hours, and at last at the mouth of night he cut another head from the Beast. And the crags echoed with the monster's rage as, in white spray like spindrift, it disappeared beneath the waves.

Again he put the head on a rope and gave it to the king's daughter, and rode off to see to his cattle. And again she met the general, hiding behind his bush, and he told her he would kill her if she did not say it was he who had cut off this head also.

"Oh, I will say it," said the king's daughter. "What other hero but you would have fought with the Uile-Beast?"

They went back to the palace, with the Beast's head on the general's back, and again there was rejoicing, and nobody doubted that such a strong suitor would take off the last head of the monster in the morning. When they reached the loch-side next day it all happened as before; the general slunk off to hide, and the young man on the black horse rode up with his dog, and dismounted at the side of the king's daughter.

"What is waking for you today?" she asked, as he lay down to sleep.

"Waking for me is to take the ring out of your other ear, and put it in mine," he said.

When he woke to fight the Uile-Beast this day, there was

more neighing and braying, more slupertash-slapertash, more banging and clanging than ever before; but at last he had the third head off the Beast, and it could roar no more as it sank beneath the waves. He put the head on the rope with the others, and rode home to his cattle.

When the last head reached the palace there was great rejoicing, and a wedding was arranged for the next day, between the king's daughter and her strong suitor, the general.

On the wedding morning the whole palace was astir early, everyone awaiting the arrival of the priest; but when he came, the king's daughter said she would only marry the man who could take the heads of the Beast off the rope without cutting it.

"Who can take off the heads except the one who put them on?" said the king.

The general stepped forward to try to take the heads off, but he could not, and neither could anyone else in the palace.

"Is there nobody else in my kingdom who can take the Beast's heads off the rope?" said the king, and they said there was only the herdsman, so he was sent for. Without any trouble he took each head off the rope and tossed it to the ground.

"But wait awhile, young man," said the king's daughter, "the one who took the heads off the Uile-Beast has my ring, and my two earrings."

The herdsman put his hand into his pocket and drew out the rings and put them on the table.

"You are indeed he," said the king's daughter.

The king was not too pleased when he found it was the herdsman who was to marry his daughter, but he had given his word, so he ordered new clothes to be brought for the young man.

"I have a wedding suit better than anything in your palace," said the herdsman, and he brought out the suit of gold he had taken off the second giant, and because he had grown so tall and strong he was able to wear it with little alteration. And that very evening he and the king's daughter were married.

So they were happy for a long time, but one day while they walked together by the side of the loch, another Uile-Beast rose suddenly from the water, and snatched the king's daughter away. What sorrow there was in the palace and the town that night, and now her husband walked up and down the loch-side, day after day and night after night, the world dark with his sadness.

One day as he paced by the loch, he met an old smith, a wise old man, and one who was often asked for his advice.

"There is but one way to kill the Uile-Beast, and the way is this," he said. "On the island in the middle of the loch is a white-footed hind, and if she could be caught a crow would spring out of her, and if the crow were caught a trout would spring out of her, and in the mouth of the trout there is an egg, and in the egg is the soul of the Beast. Break the egg and the Uile-Beast will be no more."

The young man looked across to the island, and he wondered how he would reach it, since the Beast would sink any boat that was put on the loch. In the end he decided to try to leap the channel on his black horse, and this he did, with his dog beside him. As soon as they landed they saw the hind, and the dog began to chase it, but when the dog was on one side of the island, the hind on its white feet had sprung to the other.

"Oh, it would be well if the great fox of the sheep's carcass were here now," sighed the young man, and as soon as the words were out, there by his side was the great fox. It sprang after the hind, and in a moment had brought it to the earth, and from the hind's mouth fluttered a crow. The crow flew straight up into the sky.

"Oh, it would be well if the gray hawk of the bent talon and swift wing were here now," sighed the young man, and as soon as the words were out, there by his side was the gray hawk. She shot up into the air after the crow, and in a moment had brought it to the earth. As the crow touched the ground by the waterside, out of her mouth slipped a trout which swam away into the loch.

"Oh, it would be well if the otter with the water-webbed legs were with me now," sighed the young man, and the words were hardly spoken before the otter was by his side. She dived straight into the loch, and brought the trout to the bank, and out of its mouth fell the egg. The young man leapt forward and put his foot on it, and at that instant the Uile-Beast let out a terrible roar.

"Do not break the egg, I will give you what you want," it bellowed.

"Give me back my wife," said the young man, and in the blink of an eye, there was his wife at his side. He took her hand in both of his, and then he trampled on the egg, and the Uile-Beast was dead. She was a horrible sight to see as she sank for the last time beneath the water, with her many heads, and her hundreds of eyes, and they were glad to turn away and leave her.

There was joy and laughter in the palace that night, and the young man told the king also the story of his killing of the two giants, and the king was amazed, and heaped honors on his head. This was no longer the poor fisherman's son who had married his daughter, but a prince in his own right. Sometimes the young man thought of his old father, the fisherman, and of his two brothers and his mother, but he was too busy and too happy to worry about them for long.

One day he and his wife were walking together by the side of the loch, when he noticed a small castle in a wood nearby. He asked his wife who lived in it, and she said that nobody went near the castle, for if they did they knew they would not return to tell the tale.

"Things cannot remain like that," he said. "This very night I will go and find who is the owner of the castle."

"Do not go, do not go," she pleaded. "No one ever went to the castle and came back."

"All the more reason for me to solve the mystery," he said, and she could not dissuade him.

So at the mouth of the night the young man saddled his horse, and rode to the castle in the wood, his dog at his side. When he reached the door, he saw an old crone standing there to welcome him. She rubbed her hands and smiled in a flattering way.

"Welcome to you, oh son of the fisherman, I am happy indeed to see you," she wheezed. "It is a wonderful honor to this kingdom that you have come to it, and to my little house that you have visited it. Go ahead of me, oh prince, and rest yourself inside."

The young man went in, and as soon as his back was to her, she drew her Slacken-Drudeck, her witch's wand, and hit

19

him with it on the back of the head, and his dog too. They both fell to the ground, and the black horse galloped back to the palace with an empty saddle. There was wailing in the palace that night, and there was also sorrow in the home of the old fisherman, for one of the trees behind the house began to wither.

The second son of the old fisherman saw that the tree was fading, and he told his father that his brother must be dead. He made a vow that he would go and seek out his brother's body, and mounted on his black horse, with his dog by his side, he set off in his brother's footsteps (for each of the fisherman's three sons had a horse and a dog born from the three grains that the sea maiden had given him). Up hill and down dale rode the second son, until at last he reached the palace of the king, and there they told him what had happened to his brother.

He knew that he must go to the castle in the wood, hard or easy as his errand might be; and indeed it turned out to be hard, because as soon as he entered the door, the old crone struck him with the Slacken-Drudeck, and his dog also. When his riderless horse returned to the palace there was sorrow, and there was wailing also in the house of the old fisherman when the second tree began to wither.

So the third son set out on his black horse with his dog beside him, to discover what death had overtaken his two brothers; and he did not pause till his dog had led him to the king's palace. They were happy to see him, but they begged him not to go to the black castle from which his brothers' horses had returned riderless. He told them he had vowed to find his brothers' bodies, and sadly they watched him ride off to his doom.

When the third son reached the castle the old crone met him at the door, greedily rubbing her hands together.

"Welcome to you, oh son of the fisherman," she wheezed, "happy I am to see you. Come into my humble home and rest yourself."

"Go ahead of me, old woman," answered the young man, "I do not care for flattery out-of-doors."

The crone went ahead of him through the door, and he drew his sword and cut off her head; but the sword flew out of his hand, and the old woman caught her head and put it back as firmly as it was before. The dog leapt at her, but she struck it with her Slacken-Drudeck and it fell at her feet, and this enraged the fisherman's third son. He snatched her wand from her and hit her over the head with it, and in the blink of an eye she was on the ground.

Inside the castle he came upon the bodies of his two brothers, and with one tap from the Slacken-Drudeck they were on their feet, and their two dogs with them. Then what treasure they found, gold and silver in heaps, jewels each more precious than the last. They carried it back to the palace where the king's daughter was happier to see her husband again than all the jewels. As the king was growing old he handed over his kingdom to his daughter and her husband, and for a year and a day his two brothers stayed with him to share his happiness.

Then they mounted their black horses, and with the witch's treasure behind them, and their dogs by their sides, they rode back to their father the old fisherman. He never had to work again, and as far as I know they are all living happily still; and so is the sea maiden, for the best of the jewels from the crone's castle were given to her by the old fisherman, to thank her for all she had done. Under the gleaming sea the diamonds and emeralds shone more brightly than in the air above, and she is still to be seen by lucky seafarers, sunning herself on rocks with her water-bright gems around her dripping neck.

THE SPORRAN
FULL OF GOLD

❦

Before this there was a man who had two sons, and when their mother died he married again. After a year the youngest son went to his father and said:

"Father, we will go into the world and seek our own living, for our stepmother is not good to us."

Their father wept, but he blessed them, and they walked off into the world. Soon afterward they passed by some bushes, and out of the bushes flew a bird more beautiful than anything they had seen before. They ran and caught the bird, and the younger boy tucked it under his arm, and just at that moment they met a gentleman standing at the end of his house.

The gentleman asked what bird the boy had under his arm, and he handed the bird over and the gentleman plucked a feather from its breast. On the feather was written that whoever kept it close to his heart would find a sporran full of gold every morning when he rose.

"What will you take for the bird?" said the gentleman.

"I don't know," said the younger boy.

"Will you take five pounds for it?"

"Certainly we will," said the boys, for it seemed a lot of money, even for a bird so beautiful. But it did not seem a lot to the gentleman for a bird so magical, and he asked the boys to come into his house and warm themselves, and take food in his kitchen. He took the bird and put it in a cage with the feather he had plucked from his breast, until he should make a purse in which to put it for safety.

22

The boys fed and rested themselves, and as they were leaving the house they went to have a last look at the bird in its cage, and the younger boy saw the feather and took it and put it under his shirt to remind him of their lucky sale. Then they set off happily into the world, traveling until the mouth of the night, when they stopped at the cottage of an old woman to ask for shelter.

When they rose in the morning and went to their food, the old woman found a sporran full of gold under the pillow of their bed. She hurried to them and she said:

"You are young boys to be traveling the world. Have you been to school?"

"No, we have never been to school," said they.

"Would it not be better to stay here and have some schooling?" she asked.

"Who, then, will give us food?"

"I will give you food," she said. "I am a lonely old woman and I would like your company."

So they stayed with the old woman, but at the end of a year they said that now they knew enough, and must go.

"Since you must, I will not stop you," said the old woman. "But I have something to tell you."

"What is that?" said they, because they knew nothing of the gold she had found each morning.

"One of you is possessed of a magical gift," she said. "Do you know which one has this gift?"

"No," said they.

"Stay here tonight then, and let one of you sleep one end of the bed, and the other the other end, and we will know in the morning which of you it is."

Next morning the sporran of gold was under the pillow of the younger boy, but he did not connect it with the bird's feather he always carried inside his shirt. They were both amazed to see the chest full of gold the old woman had collected, and she made them dip their fists in and take as much as they could carry, and they left a blessing with her and said farewell.

They traveled on and on, and with part of the gold they bought some good clothes, until at last they came to the palace of the king of the country. The elder boy was very handsome, and as he strolled with his brother past the palace in his blue silk suit, the king's daughter saw him. She sent a messenger after the boys and they were brought back to the palace, and the king's daughter would not be satisfied until she had the eldest boy as her husband. He was happy too, and a great wedding was held, but afterward the younger brother felt lonely.

"I will get myself a wife as well," he said. "I will choose a poor girl and make her rich with my gift." By this time he understood that it was the feather next to his heart that brought him a sporran full of gold each morning, and he was happy when the daughter of a poor widow who lived near the palace said she would marry him.

The girl and her mother were even happier when they found that gold flowed from the man of the house, that each morning he appeared with a sporran full of it.

"Where does your husband get the gold?" the widow asked her daughter.

"I do not know," she replied, "I have seen no trunk or chest in which he could keep such a store."

"Try and find out," said her mother, so the girl went to her husband and asked him the source of his gold.

"Do not worry where it comes from," said he, "as long as I give it to you."

But the girl did worry, and she worried him every day until at last, to get some peace, he told her it was from the feather he carried next to his heart. The girl told her mother, and while the boy slept they stole the feather. The girl put it next to her own heart and from then on it was she who got the gold, and after three days she threw her husband out of the house, saying she would support him no longer. Then she built herself a beautiful white house with the money from the feather, and she and her mother lived there in great style, but her husband had to beg a roof from a miller who lived near the sea.

"You poor man," said the miller's wife when she heard the story. "But I will tell you what to do. Go to your wife's house after dinner when she is taking a walk, enter her house from the back, and in the first room you come to you will find a great black hood hanging. Take it, and when your wife comes through the door, thrust the hood over her head and wish yourself and her wherever you would like to be, and your wish will come true."

The young man thanked her, and did as she told him. He found the black hood, and as his wife came through the door he thrust it over her head and wished himself and her on the Green Island at the rim of the world. In a flash they were both of them on the island, and he kept the black hood on himself, ready to fly back home again.

"I shall leave you here, for this is what you deserve," he told her. "And before I leave you I shall take the feather from next to your heart."

"Since you are to leave me, reach me two apples from that tree," his wife begged. "I have a great desire for them and I cannot get them for myself."

It seemed a small thing to do, but as he went up the tree to get the apples, the hood blew off in a puff of wind, and his wife caught it. She put it on, and she wished herself home, and there the young man was, alone on the Green Island at the rim of the world. To comfort himself he plucked two of the red apples that his wife had wanted, and ate them, and at once he felt a strange pricking sensation in his hair. Soon it felt as if there was a great weight on his head, and he put up his hand and discovered that a pair of huge deer's antlers had sprouted from him.

He wandered across the island, hardly able to carry the weight of the antlers, and when he came to another apple tree he thought he might as well eat another apple, though this one was green. As soon as he ate the green apple the antlers fell off his head, and he was able to lift his head, and for a while he felt happy. Then he began to be hungry again and started to look for something other than apples to eat.

Wandering by a stream he saw a bank of red cress which looked appetizing, so he tried a little, and at once his arms and legs turned into hairy haunches and knees, at the end of which were pointed hoofs. He was a horse, and for a long time he walked gloomily about the island, cropping at the grass like a horse, but knowing with a man's mind that this was not his real shape.

One day, while grazing by a stream, he happened to take a mouthful of green cress, and at once he was himself again. Then he found his handkerchief and he put some of the green cress in it, and some of the red, and some green apples and some red apples, which he planned to take home with him. But how was he to get home? The island was silent when he asked out loud for help; when he shouted, he knew there would be no answer.

But to his great surprise there was an answer, and he saw a boat offshore, the men on it shouting with fear, and making haste to row away as fast as they could. They thought it must be the Devil himself on the island, for what human being could live there alone?

"Do not leave me," he shouted. "Do not be afraid."

"How did you get to this place?" they shouted back.

"By witchcraft. Come for me and I will tell you."

So after a little hesitation the boat came ashore, and took him aboard, and with oars and sails they drew away as fast as they could from the Green Island at the rim of the world. When they reached the mainland the young man did not stop until he came to his own country, and the town in which his wife lived. She had grown into a great lady with the money from the sporran full of gold, with servants and a horse and carriage, and she and her mother often laughed to think of the man who had been her husband, on the island at the rim of the world.

The first thing the young man did was to buy a basket, and in it he put the green apples and the red, and the red and green watercress. Then he set out for the grand white house in which his wife lived. Outside the house he stopped and held up his basket, and the apples in it glowed like jewels.

His wife put her head out of the window.

"How much are those apples you are selling?" she asked.

"I have two kinds," he answered, holding up the basket in front of his face. "Some are for ordinary people, but these red ones are for great ladies only, for they are the sweetest in the world. The red ones are five pounds each."

His wife sent down a servant with money for one of the red apples, and the servant carried it back to her and at once she took a bite to try its sweetness. Instantly huge antlers sprouted from her head, so large that she could not raise it, and was stuck in the window screaming for help. People came running, but nobody could think what to do; indeed they stood in the street and laughed at her.

She screamed, and they laughed, and after some time a man came and shouted at her from below:

"That is a sad state you are in, oh woman. Is it a long time since it happened?" This was her husband, but he had grown a beard since he had been on the Green Island and she did not recognize him, nor did she know that it was the same man who had sold her the apple, for he had thrown away the basket.

"No, it is not long," she wailed. "But I cannot stand it much longer."

"What would you give to the man who could take those antlers off?" he asked.

"I would give him whatever he asked," she said.

"Would you give him what was closest to your heart?"

"I would give him that," she said.

So the young man took a green apple and gave her a bite, and at once the antlers fell off. Then his wife recognized him, and she was afraid.

"Now I want what is closest to your heart," he said, but she did not wish to give him the feather.

"Come to dinner tonight," she told him. "I will give you a great feast and afterward I will give you the feather."

She wanted time to consult with her mother how to get rid of her husband, because she did not intend to give him the feather. She still had the magic black hood, and they would wish him farther than the Green Island at the rim of the world as soon as the right moment came.

That evening the young man went to dinner in the white house, and there was a great feast as he had been promised, and dish followed dish, each one better than the last.

"This is splendid food," he said. "But I have something here that makes all other food tasteless in comparison," and he brought out the red watercress.

His wife and mother could not wait to try the red cress, and as soon as it had passed their lips they turned into two gray fillies. He drove them, neighing and kicking, to the miller's house by the sea, and gave them to the miller to use for bringing up the seaweed for his land, and any other dirty jobs he had. The young man did not have the magic feather, but he had the great white house and it was filled with gold, and soon he married a kind girl and as far as I know they and their children are living happily in the white house still.

THE OLD GRAY MAN
OF SPRING

There was a poor man before this, who lived on the ragged moors, and who was always doing his best to fill a sack of meal for the mill. He dug, and he sowed, and he dug again, so that they called him The Old Digger, and his wife, who was little and wrinkled, they called The Shriveled Beetle, Corrie Crisosag.

Corrie Crisosag used to spin the wool they got from their few sheep, but she never spun more than one hank of wool, and often she would throw it into a corner saying: "Off you go, you silly hank, I'm sick of the sight of you."

This was not much help to her husband, and every so often, as winter grew closer, he said: "Are you thinking of going to the weaver soon?" She would answer: "Oh, yes, I will be going soon," but still there was only one hank of wool, and as often as not it was lying in a corner.

But there came a day when Corrie Crisosag took a sack and filled it almost to the top with peats, and on them she put her hank of wool, and off she went to the weaver's. As she drew near his house, she saw his cow grazing near a waterfall. She went over to the cow and she drove it into a bog, and when it was firmly stuck she started to clap and shout and wave her arms in the air.

Out from his house the weaver came running, and when he saw the cow in the bog, he called for a man to help, and they began to heave the cow out, and Corrie Crisosag went with them and heaved too. The cow was slowly sucked out of the bog, and the weaver thanked her for her help and started toward the

31

house, but was stopped by Corrie Crisosag shouting, and calling, and clapping her hands together.

"Look at my sack," she cried, "I left it full of hanks of wool, and somebody has taken the wool out and filled it with peats."

The weaver looked at the sack, and indeed it was full of peats, and he felt ashamed that somebody should have done this to an old, wrinkled woman on his property, so he said he would weave her a piece of cloth out of his own wool in place of her stolen hanks. And Corrie Crisosag went home very happy.

After a week the weaver had the cloth ready, and Corrie Crisosag went to collect it, and put it on her back, and started home. As she was nearing the house she saw a Hooded Crow standing on a peat stack, shouting his head off.

"Gawrak, gawrack," called the Hoodie, which means "Silly woman, silly woman," but Corrie Crisosag thought he was saying: "I am the fuller, I am the fuller" (which sounds the same in Gaelic). Well, Corrie wanted a fuller, to make her cloth smooth and ready to sew into a cloak, so she went up to the peat stack.

"If that's what you are," she said to the Hoodie, "here is my cloth, full it for me," and she left the cloth there and went home.

When her husband, The Old Digger, heard what she had done he shook his head sadly. "What is to become of us?" he sighed. "You will never have any sense, Corrie Crisosag."

They had no warm cloaks for winter, but The Old Digger worked away, and he managed to earn enough to buy a carcass of meat. He cut it into small pieces, one piece for the pot each day, so that he knew they would have enough to last till spring.

Corrie Crisosag looked at the pieces of meat, and then she gathered them together and took them out to the back of the house where they had a patch of kale. She tied one piece of meat to each of the kale plants, and felt very satisfied when she thought that all she would have to do was to cut the kale and put it into the pot with the meat each evening.

When The Old Digger came home that night, he heard a strange noise from the back of the house.

"What a snarling and a barking there is from the yard," he said.

"Ah, that is very likely," said Corrie Crisosag. "They must be eating my meat."

"What meat?" he asked. "Who is eating it?"

"The meat you put in the barrel," said she. "I took it out and tied a piece to every kale plant so that I could put them into the pot together. The dogs must have found it."

"What is to become of us?" he sighed. "You will never have any sense, Corrie Crisosag. The meat has gone to the dogs, so you will have to save every piece of butter you can from the milk, and I will put it in a jar until the old gray man of spring comes along. That will have to be our food in the place of the meat."

So Corrie Crisosag filled a jar of butter, and for some time it stayed safely on a shelf. Then one day she saw an old man hobbling down the road.

"Are you the old gray man of spring?" she called to him.

"Who else?" he called back, being deaf and very tired.

"Well, if that's who you are," she said, "there is a jar of butter which I was told to keep until you came. You had better take it."

The poor old man was naturally delighted and went off happily with the butter, and when her husband came home Corrie Crisosag said to him:

"The old gray man of spring came today."

"That isn't possible," said he. "The time for spring isn't yet."

33

"He came," said Corrie Crisosag. "And I gave him the jar of butter."

"You will never have any sense, Corrie Crisosag," said he. "I am tired of you, I shall leave you and go out into the world."

"I will come with you," said she.

"If you must, you must," said her husband. "Come now, and put the door behind you once and for all."

So Corrie Crisosag took the door off its hinges and put it on her back, and trudged behind her husband into the world. At the mouth of the night they came to a wood, and The Old Digger thought it would be better if they went to the top of a tree to be safe from wild animals. So they took the door up a tree, and laid it across a branch, and the two of them sat on it, feeling rather cold and lonely.

They had not been sitting there long, when three robbers came to the foot of their tree, dragging a cow they had stolen

and killed. They put the meat into a big cauldron, lit a fire under it, and waited for it to cook. The smell of the boiling meat rose to the top of the tree, and Corrie Crisosag's mouth watered, because she was hungry as well as cold. She edged nearer to the side of the door on which they were sitting to peer down on the robbers, and the door tipped over, and she and the door and The Old Digger went tumbling down together.

The robbers heard a splintering crash, saw a pile of bodies and pieces of wood hurtling down on them, and thought it was the Devil himself. They leapt up and took to their heels, leaving the cauldron of meat behind in their fright. Corrie Crisosag and The Old Digger were left with a huge stew to themselves, and as they ate Corrie was so happy that she started to sing.

"Have you lost your reason, woman?" said her husband. "Singing at a time like this?"

But Corrie sang and sang, and her voice echoed in the dark wood, and the robbers heard it.

"That is very fine singing," said one of the robbers. "Let us go back and see if it is a devil, or if some other person is the singer."

So they went back, and when they saw a man and a woman sitting by the fire, eating the meat, they took heart and stepped forward from the darkness.

"That is a very fine song, and you are a very fine singer, oh woman," said one.

"That is true," said Corrie Crisosag. "Now I have a fine voice, but it was not always so."

"What made it so fine?"

"My tongue was scraped," said Corrie Crisosag.

"If my tongue is scraped," said the robber, "will I sing as well as you?"

"You will for sure," said Corrie.

"Will you scrape my tongue then?"

"I will for sure," said Corrie.

The robber put out his tongue, and Corrie took her knife to scrape it, and instead she cut off the end. The robber let out a yell and galloped off into the forest, calling "Bliu, bliu" because that was all he could say, and the others went after him because they thought the old woman must be a witch, if she wasn't the Devil.

But The Old Digger and Corrie Crisosag went home, carrying the cauldron with them, and they had plenty of meat for the winter. Corrie became a wise woman after that, and her husband never needed to sigh and say, "You will never have any sense, Corrie Crisosag."

HOW
THE GREAT TURISGALE
MET HIS DEATH

There was a king of Erin before this, and one day, when he was sitting on a green hillock, behind the wind and before the sun, a huge man came riding up on a shaggy blue filly.

"Who are you?" said the king.

"I," said the giant, "am the Young Turisgale, son of the Great Turisgale. Will you come and play a game of chess with me tomorrow, oh king?"

The king said he would, and in the white morning he rose early, and he went to the hillock, and there he met the Young Turisgale and they sat down together to a game of chess.

The game went to the king, and the giant asked him what he wanted for the winning of it.

"I would like that brown rough-skinned girl who is your servant," said the king, for the girl looked sad and hungry.

When the king got her home he dressed her in silks and combed her hair with golden combs and she became beautiful, and in a short time he married her. When they were married she said to him one day:

"Go tomorrow to the green hillock, and play a game with the Young Turisgale. If you win, ask as the price of your winning the shaggy blue filly he rides."

So in the white morning the king rose early, and went to the hillock and met the giant, and they played a game of chess together, and the game went to the king. The giant asked what he would take for the winning of the game.

"I would like that shaggy blue filly you ride," said the king, for the filly looked thin and neglected.

When he got her home he washed her, and brushed her, and she became a beautiful horse, fit for a king.

"Now," said his wife, "go and play another game with the Young Turisgale tomorrow. This time you will lose the game, and for your loss the Young Turisgale will put you under a spell to discover how his father, the Great Turisgale, met his death. But you will put him under a spell in return, to lie on his elbow on the green hillock until you return."

So in the white morning the king rose early, and went to the hillock, and met the giant, and this time it was a sad game for the king because the Young Turisgale won.

"What will you take for the winning of the game?" said the King of Erin.

"For the winning of the game I put you under crosses and spells, to find out how my father the Great Turisgale died and to bring back to me his Sword of Light."

"Then in return I put you under crosses and spells, to stay lying on your elbow on this green hill till I return," said the king.

He left the young giant lying on his elbow, and went home to his wife.

"Now," said she, "mount the blue filly and ride to the Kingdom of Greece, because it is there you will learn how the Great Turisgale met his death. The people will know who you are and will come to meet you when they see the filly."

Next morning the king mounted the blue filly and set off. He went swiftly, happily, without stopping, until he reached the castle of the Black Knight. The Black Knight recognized the filly, and came to welcome him, and a dove was called onto both of

39

the king's shoulders, and food was brought for him, meat of each meat, drink of each drink, warm water for his feet.

"Have you news of my sister who was taken away by the Young Turisgale?" asked the Black Knight, and was overjoyed to hear that his sister had been rescued and was now the wife of this handsome king. He took the king into his castle for the night, and in the morning he rose early to see him on his way.

"Now," said the Black Knight, "there is a river before you which you must cross to reach the Kingdom of Greece. Take with you these nine bottles of wine and these nine wheaten loaves. When you reach the river give your filly three loaves of bread and three bottles of wine, and comb her against the hair, and with the hair. If she will not jump the river, give her more bread and wine until she jumps."

The King of Erin thanked the Black Knight, and they left blessings with each other, and he left.

He traveled swiftly, happily, without stopping, until he reached the river. Then he dismounted from the filly, and fed her three loaves of bread and three bottles of wine, and combed her against the hair and with the hair. Then he tried to make her jump the river, but all she would do was dip her head in it.

He dismounted and gave her three more loaves of bread and three more bottles of wine and combed her against the hair and with the hair, and this time when he tried to make her jump she would go no farther than her belly. Again he dismounted and gave her the last three loaves and the last three bottles and combed her against the hair and with the hair, and this time he put a spur to her and she jumped dry-footed.

The young King of Greece saw him coming and recognized the blue filly, and he and all his people welcomed the king with great rejoicing. When they had feasted and drunk, the king asked how the Great Turisgale met his death, and where was his Sword of Light.

"It is a long story," said the young King of Greece. "But if you have patience I will tell it to you."

He sat the king his visitor down in a golden chair, and he himself took a silver chair, and then he began his story.

"The old King of Greece, my father, had three sons. When they were young his wife died, and he married again. But the stepmother was not only wicked, she was a witch, and she turned the three boys into wolves, and drove them to the mountains. Then she started to send round word that there were three wolves who were killing her sheep, and ordered bloodhounds and terriers to the mountains to chase the wolves.

"Two of them were chased far away, but the third went and hid in the nest of an eagle, and the bloodhounds did not find him. For nine days the wolf crouched in the eagle's nest, lying very still and eating pieces of meat the young eagles left, and on the tenth day he saw a ship passing below the crag on which was the nest. He stood up and gave a great howl, and the captain of the ship looked up and saw him. It was such a strange sight, a wolf howling from an eagle's nest, that he told two of his men to take a small boat and go and see what was happening. The boat came quite close to the shore and the wolf dropped into it, and the two men quickly tied up and took him back to the ship.

"At first the men on the ship wanted to kill the wolf, but the captain felt sorry for the mangy, half-starved animal.

" 'Let the creature be, it is without vice,' said he, and ordered food for the wolf, and loosed the ropes from round its legs. When they saw that the wolf was quiet and gentle, the sailors were glad to have him on the boat and made a pet of him, so that by the time they reached harbor he was strong and shining.

41

They took him to the palace of the King of Greece, and the king was so pleased with the gentle shining wolf that he bought him from the captain and made a palace pet of him instead.

"For a time all went well, the wolf was fed and allowed to roam the palace grounds, and everyone treated him kindly. Then the day came when the new queen had her first child. There were three nurses watching over the baby, but on the third night they slept, and a great Hand came through the window and plucked the baby from his cradle. But the wolf was chained to the bed, and leapt forward, breaking his chain, and tore off the Hand with his teeth. He and the Hand fell to the floor together, but another Hand had taken the baby away. All he could do was to take the one he had and hide it under the bed.

"When the nurses woke and saw the empty cradle they shouted and clapped their hands, pointing to the wolf with his broken chain and bloodstained mouth. The king and the queen came running, and they thought the animal must surely have eaten their child. The king ordered him to be killed in the morning, and a great fire was lighted on which to burn him. Crowds of people collected, but when the wolf was led out they were amazed to see in his mouth a great Hand. The wolf laid the Hand at the feet of the king, and at once he knew what had happened and unloosed the chains from around the animal's neck.

"Now the King of Greece had only one thought—to set out and find the giant whose hand the wolf had bitten off, the thief of his only child. So he ordered a small boat to be made ready, and gave her prow to the sea and her stern to shore, hoisted her speckled sails, and was away on the early tide. Before long he saw an island and steered toward it. When he had landed he made his way to the great gray castle that stood on a cliff above the bay.

"He approached the castle quietly, and peered in at one of the windows, and who should he see but the giant, the Great Turisgale, asleep on the floor, and his own child beside him. Above the giant's head was a shelf, and on it the Sword of Light.

"Carefully, silently, the king climbed through the window, and crossed to the sword, and lifted it from the shelf. Then with one blow he cut off the head of the Great Turisgale. Taking the sword, the giant's head, and a magic wand—and his precious child strapped to his back—he set sail for his own kingdom.

"Great was the welcome he received, and great was his joy when he struck the wolf with the magic wand and turned him back into the shape of a man. That man was me, and at the sight of me the queen went pale and fled from the kingdom. Tell the Young Turisgale that is how his father the Great Turisgale met his death. My own father too died in the fullness of time, and I became king in his stead. You shall have the Sword of Light and with it you may be able to kill the giant's son, the Young Turisgale."

The visiting king thanked the King of Greece for his story, and for the Sword of Light, and they blessed each other. Then mounting the blue filly the king traveled swiftly, happily, without stopping, until he reached his own kingdom. He was at the house of the Black Knight in no time, and the knight welcomed him as before, with food and drink and warm water for his feet.

"When you get back," said the Black Knight, "you will find a heap of bones on the green hillock. That is the Young Turisgale waiting under your spell for your return. Shout once that you have come, and the bones will start to move together. Shout twice that you have come, and the flesh will return to the bones. Shout three times that you have come, and the Young Turisgale will raise himself from off his elbow and will ask for the sword

of his father. Give the sword to him, but while you are doing it, cut off his head. If you do not do this, he will cut off yours."

The King of Erin thanked the Black Knight, and they left blessings with each other, and he rode off home. When he got to the green hillock, he shouted once, twice, three times that he had come, and the pile of bones turned back into the Young Turisgale.

"Did you find out how my father the Great Turisgale died?" asked the giant.

"I did," said the King of Erin, "I will tell you the story now. And the man who killed him gave me his Sword of Light. Here it is."

He brought out the great glittering sword and handed it to the Young Turisgale, but just as the giant's hand stretched out to take it, he flashed it instead above his head and cut through his neck with one stroke.

Then, with the magic blue filly he went home to his wife, and she and the whole kingdom rejoiced that all the Turisgale giants were dead, and would terrify the land no longer.

THE BLUE FALCON

Before this there was a king and a queen and they had one son whom they called Straight John because he was so tall and handsome, and a great hunter. When the boy was nearly grown, the queen his mother died, and the king married another wife. There was never a day when Straight John would not be out with his bow and arrow, and always he would return with game on his belt, until one day when he went to the hunting hill and got no game at all.

He could not understand why this should be, until a blue falcon flew past, as swift as one of the arrows from his bow. He shot at her, but all he got was one feather from her wing, and he put this into his hunting bag and took it home. When he arrived at the palace, his stepmother said to him: "Where is your game today?" and he put his hand into his hunting bag and found the blue feather and gave it to her.

His stepmother took the feather in her hand, and then she lifted her eyes to him and said:

"I am setting it as crosses and as spells, and as the decay of the year on you, that you be not without water in your shoe, and that you be wet, cold, and dirty, until you get for me the bird from which that feather came."

And Straight John looked at his stepmother and he replied:

"I am setting it as crosses and spells on you, that you be standing with one foot in the castle and the other in the palace, and that your face be toward the tempest whichever wind blows until I return."

46

Then without further ado he prepared for his journey, to search for the bird from which the feather came, leaving his stepmother enspelled, her face to the tempest, until he returned.

The world was wide, and everywhere he searched for the Blue Falcon, but he could not find her. Night came on, and the small brown birds were fluttering from the tree tops to rest at the roots of the thorns, and when the waste world was shut away from him by darkness he joined them for shelter, for he was cold and wet, and his shoes were full of water.

Then who should come along the road but the March Fox, and he said:

"You are sad, Straight John, and sad is the night on which you have come; I have nothing but one wether's foot and the cheek of a sheep, but we will have to make do."

They kindled a fire and roasted the meat and when they had eaten they slept, and in the morning the March Fox said:

"Oh Straight John, the Blue Falcon you are seeking is with the great Giant of the Five Heads, the Five Humps, and the Five Necks. I will show you where he lives, and it is my advice to you to go as his servant. Be very willing and quick, and be especially good to his birds, and it may well be that he will trust you with the falcon to feed. When you get the feeding of the falcon treat her with the greatest care until one day, when the giant is away from home, you get your chance to run away with her. But take care that not one of her feathers touches anything that is in the house, or it will not go well with you."

Straight John said he would follow the fox's advice, and when they reached the giant's house, he knocked at the door.

Shouted the giant: "Who is there?"

"It is I, a man who comes to see if you have need of a servant."

The giant opened the door.

"What work are you able to do?" he asked.

"I can feed birds and swine and cows and goats, and I can milk and feed sheep."

"It is a man the likes of you I am needing," said the giant, and he settled wages on Straight John, and hired him as his servant.

John took good care of everything the giant had, but especially he cared for the birds, the hens, and the ducks, and the giant noticed how much better they tasted, and he said he would rather have one hen to eat now than two of those he had had before.

"This servant is so good I will be able to trust him with the feeding of the falcon," he decided, and Straight John fed the Blue Falcon every day and its feathers shone even more brightly for his care. The giant was so pleased that he thought he could leave the bird in his servant's care when he was away from home.

He left the house one day to go on a hunting trip, and Straight John thought this was his chance to run away with the falcon. He took hold of her, and opened the door; and the falcon saw the light and she spread her wings to jump from his hand; and the point of one wing touched the door post. As soon as the feather touched the post, the door let out a screech, and the giant came thundering home at a run. He caught hold of Straight John and took the falcon from him.

"There is only one way for you to get her for yourself," he said, "and that is to get for me the White Sword of Light which is with the Seven Great Women of Jura."

So sadly Straight John was turned away, and went out into the waste world again, but who should meet him coming down the road but the March Fox.

"You are sad, Straight John," he said. "You did not do as I

told you. It is a sad night that you have come indeed, for I have nothing but the foot of a wether and the cheek of a sheep, but we will have to make do."

They took food and sleep, and the next day the March Fox said:

"Now we will go to the edge of the ocean."

When they had reached the sea's edge he said:

"I will stretch myself into a ship, and you must get on board, and I will sail with you to Jura. Go to the Seven Great Women and seek service of them, and when they ask what you can do, say to them that you are best at polishing iron and steel, silver and gold. When you are their servant take great care of silver and steel, and they will trust you with the White Sword of Light, and when you get the chance run off with it. But take even greater care that as you leave, the sheath does not touch anything in the house, or it will not go well with you."

So the March Fox stretched himself into a boat and carried Straight John to the Red Crag on the north side of the island of Jura, and he went to the castle of the Seven Great Women and took service with them. For six weeks he worked diligently, and the Great Women said one to another: "This is the best servant we have ever had, we can trust him with the care of the White Sword of Light." He took the sword and he cleaned it until it shone like the sun on the sea, until one day the Seven Great Women were away from home and he decided that this was his chance to run off with it. He put it into its sheath, and raised it to his shoulder, but as he went out of the door the point of the sheath brushed the lintel. As soon as the sword touched the lintel, the door gave a screech, and the Seven Great Women came thundering home as fast as their fourteen legs could carry them.

They took the White Sword from him and said:

"We will not give you our Sword of Light until you get for us the Golden Filly of the King of Erin."

So sadly Straight John was turned away, and went out into the world and back to the sea's edge, and there was the March Fox waiting for him.

"You are sad, Straight John," he said. "You did not do as I told you, and I have nothing this night but the foot of a wether and the cheek of a sheep, but we will have to make do."

They kindled a fire, and ate and slept, and the next day the March Fox said:

"I will stretch myself again into a ship, and sail with you to Erin, and you will go to the king's palace and seek service with him as a stable boy. When you get the work, be quick and careful, and keep the horses and the harness in good order, until the king gives you the care of the Golden Filly. When you get the chance, run away with her, but take care that as you go out, no part of her touches anything at the side of the gate except the soles of her feet. Otherwise it will not go well with you."

They sailed to Erin, and Straight John took service with the king, and kept watch over the horses until their skins shone like buttercups and the silver and steel of their harnesses glittered. The king had never seen his stables so well cared for, and he said: "This is the best stable boy I have ever had. I can give him the care of the Golden Filly." He handed the filly over to John, who cleaned her till her skin shone like marigolds, and fed her till she went fast enough to leave one wind behind and catch another. The King of Erin had never seen her look so beautiful before.

One day the king went to his hunting hill, and Straight John thought this was his chance to run away with the filly. He put on her saddle and bridle, and took her out of the stable; and as they were going through the gate she gave a swish with her tail and the tip of the tail touched the gatepost. As soon as the tail touched the post it let out a screech, and the king came galloping home, and took the filly from him.

"I will not give you the Golden Filly unless you fetch for me the daughter of the King of France," he said.

Sadly Straight John was turned away, and at the sea's edge he met the March Fox.

"You are sad, Straight John," he said, "for you did not do as I told you. I will stretch myself into a ship once more, and we will sail to France."

So they sailed to France, and the ship ran high up the face of a rock onto dry land. The March Fox told John to go to the king's palace and ask for help, saying that his skipper was lost and his ship run aground, and this is what John did. He told the king a wretched tale, of a great storm that had come on, his ship driven onto dry land where she still was, high on the rocks and lashed by the waves. The king and the queen and all their family listened to the story and decided to go and see the ship for themselves.

When they reached the shore it was just as Straight John had described, except that out of the stranded ship flowed strange and beautiful music. Before the king could stop her, the princess jumped on board to find what instrument was playing such music, and Straight John jumped after her. The princess ran from room to room, but when they were in one room the music was in another, and when at last they went back on deck the ship was at sea and out of sight of land.

"This is a wicked trick you have played on me," said the King of France's daughter. "Where are you going with me?"

"Ah," said Straight John, "I am going with you to Erin to give you as wife to the king, so that I may get from him the Golden Filly to give to the Seven Great Women of Jura, to get from them the White Sword of Light, to give to the Giant of the Five Heads, to get from him the Blue Falcon to take home for my stepmother, so that I may be freed from crosses and spells and from the decay of the year."

"I would rather be a wife for you," said the King of France's daughter.

When they reached Erin, the March Fox turned himself into the shape of a beautiful woman, and he said to Straight John:

"I will go to the King of Erin, and I will give him the wife he wants!"

When the king saw Straight John approaching with his hand in the hand of a beautiful woman, he took out the Golden Filly, saddled and bridled in silver, and led her to him, and John returned with the filly to where he had left the King of France's daughter. The king was delighted with his bride, until he got her back to the palace and she turned into a fox who snapped at his ankles and then ran off laughing. He decided he would never again try to steal another man's daughter for a wife.

"Now I will take you to Jura," said the March Fox, and he stretched himself into a ship and Straight John and the King of France's daughter and the Golden Filly got aboard, and they sailed off to the Red Crag at the north of the island.

When they landed, the March Fox said:

"Now I will turn myself into a horse, and I will give the Seven Great Women the Golden Filly they want!"

Straight John put on him the silver saddle and bridle, and he went to find the Seven Great Women, and when the giantesses saw him coming they came to meet him with the White Sword of Light. They gave the sword to Straight John, and he took off the saddle and bridle and handed them their gleaming gold horse and they led it home in triumph.

They were in great haste to mount the wonderful filly, and they got another saddle and bridle, and one of them mounted, and another on the back of the first, and another on her back, till one on top of another the Seven Great Women were perched on the back of the March Fox. One of them took a stick and struck the side of the fox and he leapt forward and galloped across the mountain and moor, backward and forward, until at last he bounded to the top of the highest mountain in Jura. He put his front feet to the edge of the cliff, and he kicked up his back legs, and down the mountain tumbled the Seven Great Women, and they were black and blue for so long afterward that the people of Jura forgot to be frightened of them.

The March Fox ran off laughing to where Straight John and the King of France's daughter and the Golden Filly and the White Sword of Light were waiting, and he turned himself into a ship again and they all sailed back to their own country. When they landed, the fox said:

"Now for the last time I will change my shape. I will become a white sword, and you will carry me to the Giant of the Five Heads, and I will give him the weapon he wants!"

When the giant saw them coming, Straight John and the White Sword of Light in his hand, he put the Blue Falcon into a basket and took her and handed her to John. Then he took into his empty hand in exchange the sword, and very beautiful and strong it felt. He fenced with it and slashed with it and it shone like lightning, until suddenly it bent in his hand and swept off four of his five heads. And the March Fox went off laughing, thinking that now the giant could never frighten anyone in his country again.

When he got back to where Straight John and the King of

France's daughter and the Golden Filly and the White Sword and the Blue Falcon were waiting, the March Fox said:

"Oh Straight John, son of Upright John, put the silver saddle on the filly's back and the silver bridle in her mouth, mount her and take the King of France's daughter behind you with the Blue Falcon in her hand. Then ride to your palace with the White

Sword of Light held in front of your face, the blunt edge to your nose. If you do not do this, when your stepmother sees you her deadly glance will shiver you into faggots. But if the blunt edge of the sword is against your nose and the sharp edge toward her, her enchantments will turn against herself, and it is she who will shiver and crumble."

Straight John did as the fox told him, and when he reached the palace, there was his stepmother as he had left her, one foot in the palace and the other in the castle. As he rode up she turned on him her poisonous glance, and in that instant shivered into a heap of faggots and was blown away on the wind. John was free of her and her spells forever, and he had the best wife in the world, and the Golden Filly who could leave one wind behind and catch another, and the White Sword to protect him from his enemies, and the Blue Falcon to bring him game each day.

He called the March Fox to him and he said:

"You are welcome to go through my land and take any beast you fancy, and I will tell my shepherds not to let fly an arrow at you or any of your race."

But said the March Fox:

"Keep your herds to yourself, there is many a man with wethers and sheep as good as yours and I will find meat in other places without coming to worry you."

The March Fox left a blessing with Straight John, and the King of France's daughter, and the Golden Filly, and the White Sword of Light, and the beautiful Blue Falcon, and as far as I know they are all together still.

THE WIZARD'S GILLIE

There was a farmer before this who had a lazy son, and he said to his wife:

"This boy will be good for nothing, it would be best if I drowned him."

He took the boy to the shore, but he could not bring himself to drown him, and as he stood staring out to sea he saw a boat approaching. The boat landed and a man climbed out and came over to him.

"Were you planning to drown your son?" he asked.

"It was in my mind," said the farmer.

"Leave him with me for a year," said the stranger. "I will give you twenty pounds for him and it will be better than drowning him."

"Oh, I will certainly leave him," said the farmer, delighted, and they made an arrangement that at the end of the year they would meet in the same place. The stranger would return the farmer's son and give him the twenty pounds.

A year passed, and the farmer went down to the shore, and there was the stranger with his son, grown so big and handsome that his father did not recognize him. The stranger gave him twenty pounds and said:

"Will you leave him with me for another year, and I will give you another twenty pounds?"

"Certainly I will," said the farmer, and they agreed to meet in the same place. At the end of the second year, there was the stranger on the shore again, and the farmer's son, even bigger and more handsome, and there was another twenty pounds in the farmer's pocket.

"Will you let me keep your son a little longer?" said the stranger, and the farmer said he would, but he forgot to say how long, and he forgot to get a promise from the stranger to meet him in this same place again with his son. So at the end of another year when he went down to the shore there was no boat, no stranger, no handsome son. Every day for a week he went to the edge of the sea and stared out, but no sail was in sight and when he returned each evening he and his wife wept.

At the end of the week he made ready to go out into the world to search for his son. He said good-by to his wife, and he walked and he walked, and everywhere he asked for news but there was none. Walking through the world, asking for news of every passer-by, he became tired and sad, and he was thinking of turning his steps for home. Then at the mouth of the night he met a tall man who stopped him.

"From where have you come, oh stranger?" said the man.

"I am a man searching for my son," said the farmer. "He went away more than a year ago and I have not seen him since."

"You sold him yourself," said the tall man. "How can you expect to get him back?"

"I sold him," the farmer wept. "There is no power that can return him to me."

"What would you give to the man who could tell you where your son is?"

"Whatever he desired, if it was in my power I would give it."

"Your son is living in the Great Castle you passed an hour back," said the man. "It is I myself, your son, who is speaking to you."

"Ah, you will never leave my arms again," cried the farmer as he clasped his son delightedly about the shoulders.

"Wait, do not rejoice too soon. Do you know to whom you sold your son? You sold him to a wizard, and to him I am bound. I and my companions can take the shape of any animal in the world, and in this art I am the most skilled of all. Tonight we are to be doves, every one of us, but I will be the dove with a broken feather in his tail. You will knock at the door of the castle, and the wizard will answer it. He will ask you in to have food, but you will say you will not take food or drink from him till you get your bargain. He will ask you what bargain, and you will say the dove with the broken feather in its tail. He will laugh and give you the dove, and when you have taken food with him you will take me and leave."

The farmer agreed to do as his son asked, and that evening he knocked at the castle door.

"A lucky stranger," said the wizard. "You must take food with me."

"I will not take food or drink," said the farmer, "unless I get my bargain."

"What bargain is that?"

The farmer looked around the great hall of the castle, then he pointed to the rafters.

"The dove with the broken feather in its tail," he said.

The wizard laughed, and when they had eaten he gave the farmer the dove, not knowing that it was the shape taken by his best gillie. A little way down the road the farmer freed the dove, and it turned into the shape of his son, and with great happiness they traveled on together.

"We are coming to a town," said the wizard's gillie, "and tomorrow there will be a great fair in it."

"What fair will there be?"

"There will be a dog fair, and I will change into the shape of a dog. There will be none as beautiful as me, and there will be a collar of gold round my neck. You will sell me at the fair, but when you sell me keep the collar of gold. When I have gone, throw the gold collar onto a green hillock and I will spring back into it, and you will have me and the twenty pounds you were paid for me."

Next day at the fair many people came to look at the beautiful dog with the golden collar, and when one man offered twenty pounds for it, the farmer let it go. But he kept the golden collar, and afterward he threw the collar onto a hillock, and at once his son was there, and with great happiness they traveled on together. Soon they reached another town and the wizard's gillie said to his father:

"There will be a fair in this town tomorrow."

"What kind of fair will it be?"

"It will be a fair of bulls, and I will be a bull. You will sell me, and you will get sixty pounds for me, and there will be a ring of gold in my nose. When you hand over the bull, the ring will jump into your hand, and you will throw it onto a green hillock, and a man will spring up, and the man will be me."

Next day the wizard's gillie became a bull. There was no other bull at the fair as beautiful, and there were many men looking at him. At last a man came and asked what the farmer would take for the bull, and he answered sixty pounds. The man paid him the money, and as he led the bull away the ring jumped from its nose, and when the farmer threw the ring onto a green hillock it turned into his son.

With great happiness the two of them traveled on until they came to another town.

"There will be a fair here tomorrow," said the wizard's gillie.

"What kind of fair will there be?"

"It will be a horse fair, and I will become a horse. It is I who will win all the prizes, for there will be none as swift or as beautiful. You will get six score pounds for me tomorrow, and now I have a secret to impart. Do you know who it is that is buying me each time?"

"No."

"It is the Great Wizard my master, and tomorrow you have an important task to perform. To do it, you must be sure not to sell the rein round my neck when you let the Great Wizard lead me away. On no account sell the rein."

Next day the farmer led his beautiful horse to the fair, and hundreds of people made offers for an animal so fine, but the farmer would not let it go for less than six score pounds. At last a man came up with a handful of silver.

"Here," he said. "Six score pounds for your horse."

The farmer took the silver, and he was so dazzled by the sight of it that before he had time to think or speak the man grasped the rein, jumped on the horse's back, and galloped away.

When the Great Wizard reached home he took the horse to his three daughters, each one of them keeping a great cauldron of water boiling. He handed them the horse and told them to boil it without delay.

"Are you not pitiful?" scoffed one of them. "Coming to your end in a cauldron of boiling water?"

"What end?" said the wizard's gillie. "Have you not heard that boiling water will do no harm to a wizard?"

"He knows what he says, for was he not the best of our father's gillies?" said the wizard's daughters, and they went to fetch three cauldrons of cold water. While they were gone, the

wizard's gillie rubbed his head against the door until he had loosened his bridle and rein, and then he turned back into his own shape, and was out of the door and away before the girls returned.

He ran off to the woods, and soon found himself by the side of a stream; but while he was sitting there who should come walking that way but the laird's wife. He thought it would be safer to turn himself into a trout and slip into the water, but the laird's wife caught him as he jumped off the bank, and put him in her apron. When she got home and looked into her apron there was no trout, but instead a gold ring. This was strange, but she said nothing, simply put the ring on her finger and blessed her luck.

Meanwhile the Great Wizard and his three daughters and his eleven gillies had set out to search for their prisoner, and when they came to the laird's castle they dressed themselves up as tinkers and asked for work, for they knew that the man they

were searching for was here. The laird took them to a stable, and gave them work, and when they had finished he asked what payment they wanted.

Said they: "No payment but the gold ring on the finger of your wife."

"Only a gold ring? Come to my wife's room, and you shall have it."

The laird asked his wife for the ring, and she took it off her finger, but before she could hand it to the tinkers it leapt from her hand into the fireplace. The Great Wizard and his daughters and his gillies pulled out every ember and sifted every ash, but before they reached the ring it turned into a dried pea, and jumped into a sack of peas on the other side of the room. Then, as quickly, the Great Wizard and his daughters and his gillies turned into doves, and started to gobble up the peas.

The laird's wife was astonished at the sight of fifteen doves where there had been fifteen tinkers before, and she hurried off to get a man to catch them. When she was gone the wizard's gillie turned into the shape of a red fox, and gobbled up the doves as fast as they had gobbled up the peas. So that was the end of the Great Wizard, and with the money in his castle the farmer and his son, the wizard's gillie, were able to buy themselves a farm each, and as far as I know they are living there very happily still.

THE THREE SHIRTS OF CANNACH COTTON

❧⬥❧

There was a king before this who had three sons and one daughter, and when the children were still young his wife, the queen, died. For a year or two he did not marry, but he became lonely and wanted a woman in the palace again. His only fear was that if he married a second time, his new wife would not be kind to his children.

He thought about this, and then he decided he would make a separate house for them. So that is what he did. It was a house all of glass on his hunting hill, a house

> Behind the wind
> Before the sun
> Where no one could see them
> But they could see everyone.

And when the children were happily installed in the sun-house on the hill, the king married again, and everyone was happy. Each day he went to the hunting hill, and what he shot he gave to the children; and all went well until his new wife had a daughter. As she grew, this new daughter turned out to be ugly and clumsy, and because she had rough hair and skin, and great big red wrists, everyone called her The Scabby Princess. It was not just her looks that were rough and hard either—she was hard and unkind by nature, scabby in every way.

On a day of days the king went to his hunting hill as usual, and while he was out the Yolack Urlar came to the palace. The Yolack Urlar was an old crone who lived in a tumbledown shack nearby. She told fortunes and made medicines and cast spells, and did all the other jobs of a witch. Everyone was afraid of her, for she was a great maker of mischief, and could raise a devil's wind to drown a man far out at sea beyond her sight.

This day when she met the queen she cackled:

"You foolish creature, dressed in your satins and silks, and thinking there is nobody dearer than you to the king."

"And is there?" asked the queen.

"Indeed there is. There is a sun-house on the hunting hill, and in it are three boys and a girl who live

> Behind the wind
> Before the sun
> Where no one can see them
> But they can see everyone.

They are the king's children, and they are the dearest things he possesses."

"And by what means can I bring them back to the palace and into my power?" asked the queen.

"I will tell you," said the Yolack Urlar. "When your husband the king comes back from the hunting hill, have a man watching by the door. You yourself stand behind the door with your mouth full of red wine, and when the king comes in, spit this out in front of him.

"He will ask what is the matter with you, and you will say that your heart's blood is coming out of your mouth.

"He will ask what will heal you, and you will say that he has the cure.

66

"He will ask what he has that is not yours also, and you will say there is something.

"He will promise that whatever it is, he will give it to you, and you will make him give you his hand on it.

"He will give you his hand and swear, and you will say that if his three sons and his one daughter came home, that would heal you."

Well, that evening when the king returned from the hunting hill, the queen was waiting for him behind the door as the Yolack Urlar had told her, with her mouth full of red wine. When he came in, she spat out the wine in front of him.

"What is it ails you?" said the king.

"My heart's blood is coming from my mouth," said the queen. "And I am like to die."

"Is there nothing that would heal you?" he asked, distracted.

"Yes, you have something."

"Whatever it is, I will give it to you," said the king, and he gave her his hand and swore to keep his word.

"It is your three sons and your one daughter coming home that would heal me," she said.

The king clasped his head in his hands and groaned.

"I bless you," he said. "But I curse the one who told you to ask this of me. If it were not for the fact that I have given my word I would not do what you ask. But my hand was my pledge."

So he went out and saddled and harnessed four horses, and sent servants to fetch his children and bring them home, crying and wailing, from their sun-house on the hill. They were happy to be with their father, but their stepmother and The Scabby Princess made them feel uncomfortable and unwanted.

Next day the king went to the hunting hill as usual, and while he was out the queen sent for the Yolack Urlar.

"Now I have them here, how can I best get rid of them?" she asked, for she was angry that the king's children were so handsome, and her own daughter so big and ugly.

"If I get sufficient payment, I will get rid of them fast enough," said the Yolack Urlar.

"What payment would you need?"

"I would need my two ears filled with wool, and my little black bag filled with meal, and enough butter to thin the meal."

"And how much would that be?"

"To fill my ears with wool would take the sheep of seven sheep houses seven years, and to fill my little black bag with meal would take the grain of seven granaries for seven years, and butter to thin it would take the milk of seven cow sheds for seven years."

"It is a great deal," said the queen. "But you shall have it."

"In that case, send each of the king's sons, and his daughter to me, one by one. Tell them to fetch from me a rare gold comb."

And the Yolack Urlar went off, laughing and rubbing her skinny hands together.

The queen sent for the eldest boy, and told him to go to the hovel where the old crone lived, and get from her a rare gold comb that was in her keeping. When he knocked on her door the witch smiled and stroked his hand and asked him in.

"Certainly you shall have the comb, oh son of the mother I loved and the father I cherished," she wheezed. "Many's the time I have sat by the fire in your father's kitchen, licking the pots and dishes left from your father's meals. I knew him, and your mother, before you were born, and loved them as a good

69

servant should. See, there is the comb at the foot of that bench over there."

The eldest boy went over and bent down with his back to her to pick up the comb; and she stepped forward and struck him between the shoulders with her magic wand. Immediately he turned into a lean gray hound, and with a howl leapt through the window and away.

Then the queen sent for the second boy.

"Your brother went to fetch a rare gold comb for me, but he has forgotten and gone off to do some mischief," she said. "Please go in his place."

So the second son went to the Yolack Urlar's house and asked for the gold comb for his stepmother.

"Certainly you shall have it, oh son of the mother I loved and the father I cherished," wheezed the old witch. "Many's the time I have sat by the fire in your father's kitchen, licking the pots and dishes. See, there is the comb at the foot of that bench over there."

The second son went to the bench, and while he had his back to her she struck him with her wand, and just as his brother had done he leapt from the window as a lean gray hound.

The same thing happened to the third boy, but meanwhile the girl, watching from a window, had seen her three brothers go into the witch's house, and three hounds come out. So when her turn came she was ready. When the witch reached for her wand, the girl grabbed the end of it and pulled the old woman's hand from her arm. Then without looking back she set off to look for her brothers.

She walked and she walked, and though the white clouds of day were going and the black clouds of night were gathering, there was no rest for her. At last, in a deep glen, she saw a house,

and being very tired went toward it. She looked inside, and there
was no one in the house:

> *Only a small bright fire,*
> *Only a pair of tongs,*
> *And as the coal fell down*
> *The tongs rose on their own*
> *And placed each piece back on the glowing fire.*

This was strange, and the girl went into the house and sat
down by the magic fire to wait for the owner of the house.
Presently a woman came in, dressed in a long green dress, and
greeted her kindly, and gave her meat for eating, and drink for
drinking, and warm water for her feet.

"And what news have you, oh stranger woman?" said the
lady in the green kirtle.

"I have no news," said the girl, "I was hoping to get some
from you."

"I have news, and you will want to know it. I have seen
your brothers roaming the country in the shape of three lean
gray hounds."

The king's daughter jumped up.

"Then I must be going at once, to try to find them."

"Stay just one night," said the green-robed woman. "You
need to rest."

So the girl stayed, and in the white morning she rose early,
and the green-robed woman made her food. When she had
eaten, she asked to be shown the way she must travel to find
her brothers.

"I have a shoe here," said the woman. "It will keep you
straight on the road until you reach the house of my sister.

When you arrive, turn the shoe round, and it will come home on its own."

The king's daughter took the shoe, and thanked her, and did not stop until she reached the house of the green woman's sister. Then she took off the shoe, and turned it round, and off it went home. She looked into the house, and there was no one inside:

> Only a small bright fire,
> Only a pair of tongs,
> And as the coal fell down
> The tongs rose on their own
> And placed each piece back on the glowing fire.

This was strange, and she went in and sat by the magic fire, and as before a green-robed woman came in, and gave her food and drink and warm water for her feet and made her rest for the night. She told her that the three brothers were living in a cave on a hill not far from her house.

"I have here a fine hempen rope," said the woman. "Tie this to your hand, and I will hold the other end and pull it if you should fall, for the hill is steep."

The king's daughter thanked her and tied the rope to her hand, and when she reached the mouth of the cave she loosed the rope, and it was pulled back by its owner. Then she stopped and went into the cave.

There was a table, and there were three cups on it, a small cup, a cup of medium size, and a large cup, and they were full of wine. The girl took the ring from her finger, which had been her mother's, and dropped it in the smallest cup of wine. Then she went and hid herself under a pile of birds' feathers which was in the corner of the cave.

She had not been hidden long when her three brothers, the lean gray hounds, came in. As soon as they entered the cave they took off their dogskins, and became men again, and each one picked up his cup from the table and began to drink the wine. As the youngest one tipped his cup to get the last drop, something went clang against his teeth. He put his hand into the cup and pulled out the gold ring.

"Surely," he said, "this is the ring of our mother. Where this ring is, there must our sister be too."

They soon found her under the birds' feathers, and they all kissed her and laughed to see each other again. They sat round the table and talked and talked, but it was a sad story they told her of the kind of life they had to lead, hounds when they were out, men only when they returned to the cave.

She asked if there was no way of bringing them out from under the spell the Yolack Urlar had put on them. They said there was a way, but it was so hard that they did not think she, or anyone, could manage it. The spell could only be broken if a shirt was made for each of them from the wild cannach cotton on the moors, and not a word spoken until the shirts were on their backs.

The king's daughter rose at once and said she would break the spell, and left a blessing on her brothers' heads, telling them to be patient until the work was done. Then, taking three sacks from the cave, she went straight to the moors where the wild bog cotton was growing, and plucking the down from each plant, began to fill them.

She worked so hard that before the day was ended her sacks were full, and she sat down to rest. Just then she saw a rider coming toward her. It was, in fact, the king of the country, and when he saw a beautiful girl resting in the middle of the wild, white cotton, he went to speak to her. And as soon as he looked closely at her face, whiter and softer than the cotton plants, he fell in love.

He talked to her gently and politely, but she could only nod and smile, and the more she smiled the more deeply in love he became, and it was not long before he was asking her in sign language if she would marry him. She replied in signs that since she was deaf and dumb it would not be right for her to marry anyone. But he persuaded her that this did not matter, that if she simply sat and looked at him forever, that would be enough. Because he was so handsome, and she too by this time had fallen in love, she agreed to go with him and become his bride.

So he lifted her, and the three sacks of cannach cotton, onto his horse, and they rode back to his kingdom, and there they were married, and still she never said a word. For months and months she sat and spun the cotton to make the shirts, and never spoke. When a year was nearly over her first child was born.

A nurse was brought in to watch over the child, and for a week she guarded the prince carefully, and then one night she fell into a deep sleep. The young queen was still spinning, and from her room she saw the nurse asleep, and then she saw a great hand come in at the window and snatch the child from the cradle and take it away. She jumped up and ran into the room and woke the nurse, but she could say nothing.

The nurse was afraid that the king would put her in prison for sleeping, so she cut her finger and rubbed the blood on the queen's dress, and then she went to the king.

"What a monster in disguise you have for a wife," she declared, "who would eat her own child."

"My wife could not do such a terrible thing," said the king.

"Indeed she did, look at the blood on her dress if you don't believe me."

The king did not want to see the blood and he loved his wife dearly so he said he would forgive her this time; and still she could say nothing. She had begun to weave the shirts. She wove and she wove and nearly a year went by and another child was born to her. Now two of the shirts were finished, and she brought in a different nurse, and for a week the baby was closely guarded. Then came a night when the nurse slept, and again a hand came through the window and plucked the child from the cradle, and again the nurse went to the king and complained that the mother had eaten it. The king was greatly troubled, but a second time he forgave his wife, and still she could say nothing.

For another year the young queen wove and wove, and now the shirts were almost finished. At the end of the year she gave birth to her third child, and she brought in a different nurse, and for a week the baby was closely guarded. But then, as before, there came a night when the nurse slept, and the hand came through the window and plucked the child from the cradle. For the third time the nurse went to the king and complained that the mother had eaten it.

The king's love for his wife was as strong as ever, but he knew that he must punish her for these terrible crimes, and still she said nothing. So with a heavy heart he condemned her to death, and when the day came for the hanging the whole kingdom was there to watch. They had grown to love their beautiful, gentle, silent queen, whose smiles made up for her lack of speech, and their hearts were heavy. And in amongst the weeping crowd were three lean gray hounds.

The queen was brought out and led toward the gallows, and the people were surprised to see that she carried on her arm three shirts as white as the bog cotton that streamed across the moors. Instead of going up the hill to the gallows, she walked toward the three gray hounds lying in the crowd. Then to the astonishment of everyone, she put a shirt over the shoulders of the first dog.

"May you spend happy hours in your fine spun shirt, oh brother," she said, and as soon as she had spoken the hound turned into a handsome young man.

"May you enjoy health and blessings, oh sister," he replied.

She moved to the second hound, and the third, and when all three young men had thanked and blessed her, there was laughter and singing and much to tell and explain. To complete the happiness of the queen, her brothers told her it was they who had stolen her children, because they were afraid that if she kept them she would be bound to speak, and they would never be brought from under their spell.

So the king and queen were reunited with their three little boys, and all was gladness. When the king heard the story of the stepmother and the Yolack Urlar he said he would make a great fire and burn them and grind them to powder, and let their ashes fly in the wind. But because he was a kind and forgiving king he did none of these things; but they and The Scabby Princess kept well away in case he should change his mind.

THE SHARP GRAY SHEEP

Once there was a king and a queen, and they had one daughter. The queen died, and the king married again, and the new queen was very unkind to the child of the king's first wife. She used to beat her, and drive her out-of-doors to herd the sheep, and gave her only a morsel of food. The poor princess wandered half-starving with her flock, until a certain sharp-horned gray sheep started to bring her meat. Each day the gray sheep fed her, and she grew plump and rosy, and her stepmother was angry.

She wondered how the girl could stay alive, let alone healthy, and she went to the old witch in the bothy for advice. The hen-wife said she would send her own daughter, Scabby Mary, to herd the sheep with the queen's stepdaughter, to find out where the food was coming from, so this is what she did. All day long Scabby Mary sat with the flock, and while she was there the sharp gray sheep would not come near. The princess was growing faint with hunger, and she said to Scabby Mary, "Put your head on my knee, and I will dress your hair."

The hen-wife's daughter laid her head on the princess's knee, and in a few minutes she was asleep, and while she slept the gray sheep came quietly up with the meat. But Scabby Mary, being a witch's daughter, had an eye at the back of her head, and with this eye she saw what happened, and when she woke she went straight home and told her mother. The hen-wife told the queen, and the queen decided that the gray sheep must be killed.

77

Next morning the sharp gray sheep went to the king's daughter and said to her:

"They are going to kill me, but steal you my skin, and gather you my bones, and roll the bones in the skin, and I will come alive again and return to you."

So the gray sheep was killed, but the princess collected her skin and bones, and rolled the bones in the skin. Only she forgot one little hoof, so that when the sharp gray sheep came alive she was lame. But she continued to bring meat for the queen's stepdaughter every day on the three hooves she had left, and the girl grew rosier and more beautiful, and one day a young prince who was out hunting saw her.

"Who is she?" he asked his followers, and they said she was only a shepherdess with a flock of gray sheep to watch, one of which was lame. The prince returned again, and again, and each time he saw this shepherdess with the lame gray sheep always at her side, he thought her more beautiful. But Scabby Mary saw him take the same road to the glen where the queen's stepdaughter spent her days, over and over again saw him ride into the glen in the morning and leave when the shadows were growing long, and she went and told her mother the hen-wife. The hen-wife told the queen, and when the queen discovered that a prince was spending his time with the stepdaughter she hated, she sent at once for the girl. She put the princess into the kitchen, to do all the dirtiest work, and she sent her own daughter out every day into the green glen with the sheep, hoping that the prince would fall in love with her instead.

The prince was sad when he saw the new shepherdess, who was dark and scowling, and then one day he noticed that the lame gray sheep would leave the flock in the evening and limp off by herself. So he followed her, and behind a green oak he found the two of them, the beautiful shepherdess and the lame sheep, and he gave the girl a pair of gold shoes and told her that he loved her. She took the shoes and said she would slip out of church early and meet him behind the green oak for a short while before she had to be back in the palace kitchen.

This plan worked twice—the princess slipped out from the church, and the sharp gray sheep kept watch in case she should be followed—but the third time the queen saw her go. She rose from her seat, and the princess ran so fast to get away from her, for she should not have been in church at all, that she dropped one of her gold shoes. The prince picked up the shoe from the mud and declared that he would only marry the one whom it fitted.

Quickly the queen hid her stepdaughter in a small space behind the fireplace and brought out her own dark scowling daughter to try on the gold shoe. Of course the shoe was too small for the big rough feet of the girl, but the queen was determined that it should fit, so she took her daughter to the hen-wife. The hen-wife cut off the ends of her toes, and then the shoe fitted, and the prince had to agree to marry the girl as he had promised.

When the day of the wedding came, the princess was still imprisoned in the space behind the fireplace where the queen her stepmother had kept her in case the prince should see her. All the wedding guests were gathered in the great hall of the palace when a small bird came to the window and sang:

> "The blood's in the shoe
> Of the liar, the liar,
> The foot that is true
> Is behind the fire."

"What is that bird saying?" asked one of the guests.

"What does it matter what it is saying?" said the queen. "It has a nasty, lying little beak."

Again the bird came to the window, and a third time, and sang:

> "The blood's in the shoe
> Of the liar, the liar,
> The foot that is true
> Is behind the fire."

Then the prince rose and said:

"We will go and see if what the bird says is true."

He ordered a search behind the great fireplace, and there, sure enough, was a secret chamber, and in it the princess he truly loved, wearing a single gold shoe. When the other gold shoe was brought from under the bed of the queen's dark scowling daughter it was found to be full of blood, but when it was cleaned it fitted perfectly the foot of the queen's stepdaughter.

So the true princess married her prince, and they went back to his kingdom, taking with them the lame gray sheep with the sharp horns, who lived with them in the greenest glen in the world for many happy years.

THE SON OF THE KING OF THE CITY OF STRAW

There was another time when all the birds were gathered together for war.

Said the son of the King of the City of Straw:

"I will go and see the battle, and I will bring back to you, my father, certain news of who is to be king of the birds for this year."

But when he got there the battle was over, except for one last fight between a black raven and an eagle. It seemed as if the eagle would win, and when he saw this the king's son stepped forward and with one blow of his sword took off the eagle's head. When the raven was able to draw breath, he said:

"For your kindness to me this day, I will show you the world. Come up to the root of my two wings, and hold firm to my feathers."

The king's son climbed up on the raven's back, and without stopping they journeyed over seven bens, and seven glens, and seven moors.

"Now," said the raven, "do you see that house over there? A sister of mine lives in it, and I will stand surety that you will be welcome there. When she asks you if you were at the battle of the birds, say that you were; and when she asks if you saw a black raven, say that you did; and be sure to meet me in this same place early tomorrow."

The king's son received a fine welcome just as the raven had said: meat of each meat and drink of each drink and warm water for his feet. And after he had rested in a soft bed, he met the raven next morning and they flew on. A second night they rested, when they had journeyed across seven bens and seven glens and seven moors, and his welcome was as good as before. Then a third day and night they traveled and rested, but on the fourth morning, in the place of the raven, who should meet the king's son but a handsome man, a stranger, with a bundle in his hand.

"Have you seen a great black raven?" said the king's son to the stranger.

"You will never see the raven again," said the young man. "I am the raven. I was put under spells, but it is you who have freed me from them. In return, I will give you this bundle. Turn back and travel the way you came, spending each night in the same house you stayed in before, but be sure of one thing. Do not open the bundle until you have reached the place where you most desire to live."

The king's son said good-by to the handsome stranger, and shouldering the bundle he set off back to his father's house. Each night he took lodgings with the sisters of the raven who had been enspelled, and each day started out refreshed. He had left the last house, and was trudging through a thick forest on the edge of his father's kingdom, when the bundle on his back seemed to have become especially heavy. He put it down on the forest floor, and he thought, as he was so near home, it would do no harm to open it. So he loosed the wrappings, and before he could blink an eye there in front of him was a castle more beautiful than any he had ever seen. Round the castle was a garden and an orchard full of every kind of fruit and flower. He stood in front of it and was filled with wonder and sorrow.

Too late he remembered that the raven had told him not to open the bundle until he was in the place where he most wished to live. Now he could not put the castle and the orchard back in the bundle and carry it to the green valley opposite his father's palace, but he did not want to live in it here, in the middle of a great gloomy forest. He was sitting staring longingly at the flowers and the orchards when a shadow fell across him, and he looked up to see a giant standing over him.

"Bad is the place where you have built your house, oh son of the king," said the giant.

"This is where it is, but this is not where I would wish it to be," said the king's son, and he told the giant of how he had opened the bundle against the orders of the man who had given it to him.

"What reward would you give me for putting the castle back in the bundle where it was before?" said the giant.

"What reward would you want?" said the king's son.

"I would want your first son when he is seven years old," said the giant.

"If I have a son, you shall have him," said the king's son.

As soon as he had spoken, the castle and the gardens and the orchards were back into the bundle.

"Now you take your road, and I will take mine," said the giant. "But remember your promise. If you do not remember I will."

The king's son shouldered the bundle, and in a few days he was in the place where he most desired to live, the green valley opposite his father's palace. He opened the bundle again, and there was the castle, and at the door of the castle the woman he most desired to marry.

"Come inside, oh son of the king," said the beautiful maiden. "Everything is in order, and we shall be married this very night."

Which is what happened, and after a day and a year a son was born to them, and for seven years after they were happy.

But one day the figure of a huge man was seen approaching the castle, and the King of the City of Straw remembered his promise to the giant. His father had died and he was now the ruler of the country, but he had never told his queen of the promise.

He had to tell her now.

"Leave the matter between me and the giant," said the queen.

"Bring out your son," roared the giant as he approached. "Remember your promise."

"I have remembered it," said the king. "I will give him to you when his mother has made him ready for the journey."

The queen brought out a boy, and the giant took him by the hand and they set off together while the sad mother and father wept at the castle gate. But before they had gone far the giant put a rod into the boy's hand.

"If that was your father's rod, what would he do with it?" he said.

"If that rod was my father's he would beat the dogs and cats who went to take the king's food," said the boy.

"You are the cook's son," roared the giant, and he turned back to the palace in rage and fury. When he arrived, he told the king that if he did not give him his own son, the highest stone in the palace would be flat on the ground with the lowest.

So the queen went in, and she brought out another boy, and the giant took him by the hand, and they set off together. Before they had gone far, the giant put a rod into the boy's hand as he had done before.

"If that was your father's rod," said the giant, "what would he do with it?"

"He would beat the dogs and the cats when they came near the king's bottles and glasses," said the boy.

"You are the steward's son," roared the giant, and he turned back to the palace in an even greater rage. The ground quivered under his feet and the castle shook as he approached.

"BRING OUT YOUR SON," he roared, "or in the wink of an eye the highest stone in your palace will be down with the lowest."

So the king and the queen had to give up their only son, and the giant took him home and broght him up as his own. When he was nearly grown, came a day of days when the giant was away in town, and the king's son heard music coming from the top of the house. It was more beautiful than any music he had heard before, and he followed its sound to the top of the steep stone stairs that led to the roof of the giant's castle, where in an attic room sat a girl at a harp. She was as beautiful as the music, and he was surprised when she told him she was one of the giant's daughters.

"Tomorrow you will be given the chance of marrying one of my two sisters," she told him, "but you must say you will not have anyone but me. My father has promised me to the son of the King of the Green City, but I do not love him."

Next day the giant brought out his daughters and said:

"Now, son of the King of the City of Straw, take for your wife one of my two older daughters, and you may have leave to go back to your home with her the day after the wedding."

"It is your youngest daughter I want," said the king's son.

The giant's anger blazed out.

"Before you get her, there are three things I shall require of you," he roared.

"Speak on," said the king's son.

The giant took him to the stables.

"A hundred cows have been housed here for seven years without the floor being cleaned. I am going to town today, and when I return at nightfall the stable must be so clean that a golden apple can run from end to end without receiving a blemish. If you do not do this, not only will you be without my daughter for your wife, it is a drink of your blood that will quench my thirst this night."

The king's son began at once to clean the stable floor, but it would have been as easy to pour out the ocean. At midday, with the sweat blinding him, he was in despair when the giant's youngest daughter came to him.

"You are being punished, oh son of the king," she said.

"I am indeed," said he.

"Come over here and lay your head on my knee," she said.

"There is nothing but death waiting for me," said the king's son. "I may as well rest."

He sat down and laid his head under the girl's hand, and at once fell into a deep sleep. When he awoke there was no giant's daughter to be seen, but a stable so clean that a golden apple could safely run from end to end of it. Just then the giant came in.

"You have cleaned the stable, oh son of the king," he said.

"I have cleaned it."

"Somebody cleaned it," said the giant. "And since it was such hard work, you may have until this time tomorrow to thatch it with birds' feathers, no two feathers of the same color."

Next morning the king's son was on his feet before sunrise, his bow and arrows at his side; but though he ran across the moors till the sweat blinded him, birds were hard to find. At midday the giant's daughter came out to meet him.

"You are being punished, oh son of the king," she said.

"I am indeed," said he. "I have only shot two birds all day, and both of them are black."

"Come over to this green mound and lay your head on my knee," said she.

"There is nothing but death waiting for me," he said. "I may as well rest."

He laid his head under the girl's hand, and at once he fell

asleep, and as before when he awoke the giant's daughter was nowhere to be seen. But when he returned to the stable he found it neatly thatched with birds' feathers, and the giant was soon home to see it.

"You have thatched the stable, oh son of the king," he said.

"I have thatched it."

"Somebody thatched it," said the giant. "Well, there is one more small task for you. There is a fir tree by the side of that loch, and there is a magpie's nest at the top of it. I must have the eggs in the nest for my first meal tomorrow, all five of them, and not one must be cracked or broken."

Early next morning the king's son went to the loch, and there was no difficulty in finding the fir tree. In the whole dappled wood there was no tree like it in size, for from the root to the first branch it spanned five hundred feet. The king's son went four times round the tree, and each time he tried to find some way of climbing its smooth trunk.

Just then the giant's daughter appeared.

"You are skinning your hands and feet, oh son of the king," she said.

"Indeed, I am no sooner up than down," he sighed.

"There is no time to delay," she said, and she stretched herself very tall and spread her fingers to make a ladder for the king's son to climb to the first branch of the fir tree.

After that it was not difficult for him to reach the magpie's nest, but before he was back on the ground again she said: "Make haste, for the breath of my father is burning my back." And in her own hurry to pull her hands free, the tip of her little finger was left in the tree.

"Now," said she, "go home with the eggs quickly, and your three tasks will be done. You will have me for your bride tonight if you can recognize me. My two sisters and I will be dressed in the same clothes, but when my father says, 'Go to your wife, oh son of the king,' look for a hand with the top of the little finger missing."

So the son of the king took the magpie's eggs to the giant, and was told to prepare for his wedding that very night. A great feast was arranged, and all the giant's friends and relations were there. Dancing shook the giant's castle, and music echoed from its walls, and at last the giant said:

"It is time for the choosing of the bride. Take your wife, oh son of the King of the City of Straw."

His three daughters, all dressed the same, all made to look exactly alike, were led in, and all of them held out their hands; and the king's son took the hand from which the end of the little finger was missing.

"You have chosen right," said the giant, but his voice was hard. "She is your bride."

But when the king's son and his bride went up to their room, she said:

"Do not sleep, if you do not wish to die. We must fly or my father will kill you."

So they stole out of the castle, and from the stables they took a blue filly and out of the yard they galloped. In the white morning, when they had ridden some distance, the girl said:

"My father's breath is burning my back again. Put your finger in the filly's ear, and whatever you find, throw it behind you."

"It is the twig of the sloe tree I find," said the son of the king.

"Throw it behind you," said she.

No sooner had he thrown the twig behind him than a great wood of blackthorn grew up, twenty miles thick, and so dense that not even a weasel could pass through it. The giant came thundering up and tore the hair from his head and the skin from his neck on the thorns of the wood. He had to go back for his ax and his wood knife, and when he returned the blue filly was long out of sight.

In the heat of the day, the girl said:

"The breath of my father is burning my back. Put your finger in the filly's ear, and whatever you find, throw it behind you."

"It is a splinter of gray stone I find," said the king's son, and he threw it behind him. In the wink of an eye, twenty miles of gray rock appeared, and when the giant came thundering up he could not pass. He had to go back for his hammer and his mighty mattock, and by the time he had returned and cut a hole through the rock, the filly was long out of sight.

Toward evening, the girl said:

"Again the breath of my father is burning my back. Take one more look in the filly's ear, son of the king, or we are lost."

He looked again, and drew from the filly's ear a skin bag full of water.

"Throw it behind you," said she. The king's son threw the bag of water, and at once there was a loch twenty miles long and twenty miles broad behind them. The giant came thundering up, and he was going so fast that before he knew it he was in the middle of the loch. He sank with a great splash, and that was the last they saw of him.

"Now," said she, "my father is drowned and will trouble us no more. But there is one more test for you to do alone. Go you ahead to your father's house, and say that you have me with you. But do not let any creature kiss you, for if you receive a kiss, you will forget that you ever saw me."

With a heavy heart the king's son left her, promising to return as soon as he had told his father and mother about her and about their marriage. The whole palace was full of laughter at his arrival, and his parents were particularly overjoyed, and expected to embrace him. But he gently put them away, saying that he had some important news to tell them before he could receive their kisses. Eagerly they led him to a chair to give him food and drink and to hear his news, and by the chair lay an old greyhound.

The dog lifted his head at the sound of the voice of the one who had been his master, and jumped up in joy, and licked him on the mouth; and from that moment the king's son forgot all about the giant's daughter. He allowed his parents to kiss him too, and to make plans for his marriage, for they were getting old and wished to hand over the kingdom to him.

Meanwhile the wife of the king's son sat by the side of the well where he had left her, and waited and waited. At the mouth of the night she climbed into an oak tree beside the well and fell asleep in the fork of the tree. There was a shoemaker's house nearby, and next morning when the shoemaker's wife came to fetch her husband a drink from the well, she saw the reflection of a beautiful woman in the water. She thought it was her own face she was seeing, and she threw down the pot in her hand and broke it, and went back to the house in a temper.

"Where is my water?" asked the shoemaker.

"You stupid, insignificant man, I have carried your water too long," said she. "I am too beautiful for such a task."

"You have lost your wits, my wife," said the shoemaker. "Go you, my daughter, and get a drink for your father."

So the shoemaker's daughter went to the well, but the same thing happened to her: she saw the reflection of a beautiful

93

woman in the water, a woman too beautiful to be working all day for her father. She threw down the pot and went home in a rage.

"Where is my drink?" said her father.

"Am I to be your slave?" said the girl. "Fetch your own water in the future."

The shoemaker was mystified. The well had put his wife and daughter under spells, and he must go and report the matter to the king. Without delay he set out for the palace, and was led before the throne to explain to the king about the magic water that could change his wife and daughter into different people just by looking into it.

"Is this magic in the water new?" asked the king.

"As new as this morning," said the shoemaker. "I have drawn my water from this well, and my father before me, years without number."

"Then I will send my son to see if your story is true, and if it is as you say, we will have to find stronger spells to lift those evil ones in the water."

So the son of the King of the City of Straw went back with the shoemaker to the well, and stood under the oak tree, and looked into the water. There he saw the face of the most beautiful woman in the world, the face of his wife. Memory of the giant's daughter returned, and as he gazed up into the tree he saw her laughing down at him.

"Since I did all your tasks for you, could you not do this one for me, my husband?" she said.

"It was my dog that kissed me," he replied, laughing too, "but in future all my kisses are for you."

They returned to the palace together, and a priest came to bless them, and there was great rejoicing and a feast prepared which, as far as I know, is going on still.

THE SHIP THAT SAILED
ON SEA AND LAND

There was a king before this who lived on the Isle of Bens, and he had a daughter who was extremely beautiful. As is the way of beautiful maidens, she had many suitors, but the king said she would only be given in marriage to the man who sailed a ship on sea and land. Some of her suitors tried to sail such a ship, but none of them succeeded.

There was on the island a poor widow, and she had three sons. One day the eldest son said to his mother:

"Rise, oh mother, and make me a bannock, and I will go and try to make a ship that sails on sea and land, and win for myself the king's daughter."

His mother rose, and she made two bannocks, one big and one small, and she said to him:

"Which would be the better for you, the big bannock with my curse, or the small bannock with my blessing?"

"Blessing or curse, I will take the big bannock," said her son, and he went off with it into the woods and began to build a ship.

He had not been long at the work when an old gray man came down the road, and said to him:

"You are busy, oh son of the widow."

"That I am," answered the boy.

"If you will give me some of your bannock I will help you," said the old man.

"Indeed I will not. It is small enough as it is, since it must last me until I finish this ship," said the widow's son. So the old man went on his way, and after struggling on for several days the boy gave up his task and went home.

"Well then," said the widow's second son, "since you have not made the ship, let me try."

So he asked his mother to rise up and make him a bannock, and the same thing happened to him as to his brother. He took the big bannock with her curse, and when the old gray man asked him for a share of it he refused him, and after a few days he returned home with the ship unfinished.

Then on a day of days, the youngest son of the widow said to his mother:

"Rise, oh mother, and make me a bannock, and I will go and try to make a ship that will win the king's daughter."

His mother rose, and she made two bannocks, and said:

"Now take your choice—the big one with the curse of your mother, or the small one with her blessing."

"Give me your blessing, mother," said her son, "and whether the bannock is big or small, I will be happy."

So his mother gave him the small bannock with a blessing on it, and he put his back to the town, and went into the woods to build a ship. He had not been long at work when the old gray man came down the road.

"You are busy, oh son of the widow," he said.

"That I am," said the boy.

"If you will give me a share of your bannock I will help you," said the old man.

"Oh, it is small enough, take it all," said the widow's son, so the old man ate the bannock, and then he began to help build the ship, and in no time at all it was finished. They climbed on board and away they sailed to look for a skipper, and the ship sped with the wind, and it was the same to her whether a moor or a marsh or the sea was beneath her.

As they sailed by the side of a wood, a deer bounded out and leapt along beside them, and after it came a man who caught up with the deer and held it fast.

"It is a good runner you are," said the old man. "What is your name?"

"My name is Swift Shanks."

"Then you had better come with us and be the skipper of our swift ship," said the widow's son, so Swift Shanks jumped aboard and they sailed on.

They had not gone far when they saw a man kneeling on the ground with his ear to the earth, and they stopped and asked him what he was doing.

"I am listening to the grass coming up," said he.

"It is a good listener you are," said the old man. "What is your name?"

"My name is Good Hearing."

"You had better come with us on our swift ship," said the widow's youngest son, so Good Hearing jumped aboard and they sailed on.

They had not been sailing long when they saw a man sitting on a rock which splintered under him every time he moved, and they stopped and asked him what he was doing.

"Just sitting here splintering rocks to pass the day," said he.

"It is a strong man you are," said the old man. "What is your name?"

"My name is Hard Haunches."

"Then you had better come with us on our swift ship," said the widow's son, so Hard Haunches jumped aboard and they sailed on.

They had not been sailing long when they saw a man sitting with a gun to his eye which was pointed across the sea, and they stopped and asked him what he was doing.

"I am taking aim at that bird over in Erin," said he.

"Those are good eyes you have," said the old man. "What is your name?"

"My name is Straight Aim."

"Then you had better come with us on our swift ship," said the widow's son, so Straight Aim jumped aboard and they sailed on.

They had not been sailing long when they saw a man sitting by the side of a small loch, sucking up the loch water and spitting it out again. They stopped and asked him what he was doing.

"Having a drink after my meal," said he.

"That is a wide mouth you have," said the old man. "What is your name?"

"My name is Great Gulp."

"Then you had better come with us on our swift ship," said the widow's son.

So Great Gulp jumped aboard, and they all sailed on until they came to the king's palace. When the king saw the ship coming across the green fields, and saw that it was the poor widow's son who was at the helm, he did not smile. He had no wish to give his daughter to a widow's son, even though he had built a ship that sailed on sea and land, so he called a council of his nobles.

The nobles collected from every town on the Isle of Bens, and they debated what should be done, and each of them declared that if right and justice should stand, the king must give his daughter to the widow's son. But in amongst the council sat the Yolack Urlar, the witch of the palace, and she said that there was another test for the suitor of the king's daughter before he could prove himself worthy of her. He must bring a bottle of water from the green well at the brown rim of the world faster

than her own daughter, or he must find someone else to do so. Her daughter, Black Rags, was a witch like herself and could fly like the wind.

"Let me go," said Swift Shanks, and off he raced with Black Rags. But though she went like the wind he sped like a hurricane, and reached the well before her, and filled a bottle of water.

Black Rags met him as he was leaving the well, and she thought she would get the water from him with the wiles of her tongue since she could not get it with the swiftness of her feet. "You are tired," she said. "Be seated, take breath, and I will stroke your hair."

Swift Shanks was very tired, so he sat himself down at the feet of Black Rags, and as soon as his head was laid on her knee he fell into a deep sleep. She reached for the skull of a sheep that was nearby, and she put it under his head, and then taking the bottle of water she put her heels to the ground and off she sped.

"I hear something," said Good Hearing.

"What do you hear?" asked the widow's son.

"I hear the snores of Swift Shanks. He is sleeping near the green well, and Black Rags has taken the water from him and is flying back with it."

"We will see about that," said Straight Aim, and he let fly a bullet that broke the skull of the sheep that was under Swift Shanks' head. He woke up with a start, and sped after the witch's daughter, and grabbed the bottle from her. When he reached the palace he gave the water to the king, but the king still did not smile, and the Yolack Urlar was called again.

"There is another test," whispered the Yolack Urlar to the king. "And it will finish the widow's son. Invite him to a great feast today, and make him sit in the chair with the poisoned spike. That will finish him. He will court your daughter no more."

But Good Ears heard her whispers, and that evening, when the widow's son went to the feast, Hard Haunches went with him as his servant. The king welcomed his guest, and showed him to the best chair at his table, but Hard Haunches said it was his custom to sit first in any chair in which his master was to sit. Hard Haunches sat himself down in the chair with the poisoned spike, and he broke the spike and the chair into pieces, and he himself was unhurt.

After dinner the Yolack Urlar was called again, and she said there was one more test for the widow's son to see if he was a fit husband for the princess: he must bring the loch of water at the top of the hunting hill to the glen opposite the palace or he must find someone else to do it.

"If they need water," said Great Gulp, "it may well be that I can give them enough."

So Great Gulp went up to the hunting hill, and he sucked up the water from the loch, and he poured it out onto the palace, spouts and fountains and rivers of water until the whole palace was awash, and the king begged the Yolack Urlar to tell him to stop. If he stopped, the king would arrange a marriage for that very night; and that is what he did. The witch and her daughter were not invited, but the widow came with her sons, and the chief guests were the old gray man and Swift Shanks and Good Hearing and Hard Haunches and Straight Aim and Great Gulp. It was the biggest wedding ever held on the Island of Bens, and as far as I know they are still eating and drinking and dancing in honor of the widow's son and his bride and their magic ship.

THE BROWN BEAR
OF THE GREEN GLEN

There was a king once who had three sons: the youngest was named John, and word went round that he was foolish. The king their father was struck with sudden trouble when he lost at one time the sight of his eyes and the strength of his feet, and his sons were as troubled as he was. The two elder brothers said there was only one cure for him, to fill three bottles with the water that lay on the Green Isle at the edge of the world, and straight away they set out to do so.

Foolish John thought he would go too, and at the first big town of his father's kingdom he caught up with his brothers.

"Oh my brothers," said he. "So soon we meet."

"And sooner still you had better take yourself home," said they, "or we will have the breath out of you."

"Have no fear," said foolish John, "I do not wish to stay with you."

He mounted his old white horse and rode out of the town until the shadows grew long and he found himself in a great forest.

"Hoo, hoo," said John to himself. "Night is coming on and it isn't right for me to be walking this wood alone."

He tied his lame white horse to a tree and climbed to the topmost branch. He had hardly settled himself down when he saw a bear loping up with a fiery cinder in its mouth.

"Come down, oh son of the king," said the bear.

"Certainly not," said John, "I am safer where I am."

"Then if you will not come down, I will come up," said the bear.

"Do you think I am a fool?" said John. "A shaggy, shambling creature like you climbing a tree!"

"If you will not come down I will come up," repeated the bear, and he began to crawl, hand over hand, up the trunk of the tree.

"Dear Lord, you can climb trees!" said John. "Very well, keep clear and I will come down and talk to you."

A little nervously, the son of the king slid down until he was standing on the ground beside the bear, who had taken the cinder from his mouth and was looking friendly. He asked John if he was hungry, and when he said he was the bear disappeared for a few moments and returned with a roebuck, freshly killed. He lit a fire with the cinder, and had soon roasted a haunch of the deer for John's supper.

"Now," he said when the meal was eaten, "lie down between my paws, and you need not fear cold or hunger until morning."

So the son of the king curled up between the shaggy feet of the great brown bear and slept soundly through the night. Early in the morning:

"Are you sleeping, oh son of the king?" asked the bear.

"Not a heavy sleep," said John.

"It is time to be on your feet then, it is a long road before you; two hundred miles to the edge of the world. Are you a good horseman, John?"

"There are worse than me, but my horse is old and lame."

"Loose your horse then, and climb on my back," said the bear.

John untied his old horse and it set off home; and he himself gave a spring at the back of the bear. He clutched at the shaggy brown hair, but he could not hold it and before he knew what had happened he was lying on his back on the ground.

"Bad, bad," he said as he picked himself up. "I will have to do better."

This time he used both nails and teeth, and clinging on like a burr he was carried two hundred miles without stopping, until they reached a giant's house. He slid to the ground, as fresh as when he had started.

"Now, John," said the bear, "you will stay this night with the giant, crabbed though he is. Tell him it was the brown bear of the green glen who sent you and you will not lack for food and comfort." He said good-by and shambled off, the cinder in his mouth; and rather nervously John went to the door of the giant's house and knocked.

"Son of the king!" said the giant when he opened the door. "Your coming was foretold, and since I did not get your father I will have his son. Shall I stamp you into the ground with my feet or blow you up to the sky with my breath?"

"Neither of either," said John, "because it was the brown bear of the green glen who brought me here."

"Come inside, son of the king," said the giant, "and you will have all that you need this night." And he was true to his word, for he gave John meat of each meat, drink of each drink, and

warm water for his feet, and when John had rested for a couple of days he took him to the house of another giant nearby. Here they were met by the brown bear who said to John:

"I do not know this giant well, but I know that before you have been long in his house, you will have to wrestle with him. And if you find yourself on your back, say to him that if the brown bear of the green glen was there, he would soon be his master."

So John said good-by to the first giant, and knocked on the door of the second.

"Aiee, aiee," said the giant when he saw the boy. "It is the son of the king, and if I did not get your father I will have his son."

And immediately he grabbed foolish John, and they began to wrestle. Backward and forward they stamped and heaved, enough to make a bog out of rock. Backward and forward they stumbled and kicked, sinking to the knees in the hardest ground, in the soft ground sinking to the thighs, shaking the earth so that spring water spurted from the face of the cliffs. John was knocked and bruised in every bone of his body.

"Slowly, slowly," he gasped. "If only I had the brown bear of the green glen here you would not jump so high."

As soon as the words were spoken, the bear was by his side.

"Indeed, indeed," said the giant. "Oh son of the king, now I know why you have come, better than you know it yourself. Rest and I will do what needs to be done."

Then the giant called his shepherd, and told him to bring the best wether sheep on the hill, and to kill it and put its carcass by the door.

"Now, John," said the giant, "an eagle will come and she will settle on the carcass of the wether. There is a wart on the ear of this eagle, and you must cut it off with one stroke of your sword, and not one drop of blood must you spill."

The eagle came, just as the giant said, and settled on the dead sheep and began to eat, and at once John drew close to her, and with one stroke of his sword cut off the wart from her ear without a drop of blood spilt.

"Ah, son of the king," said the eagle, "come up and sit between my wings, for I know why you have come, better than you know yourself."

So John said good-by to the second giant, and climbed up between the eagle's wings, and with a great flap they were up, now over the land, now over the sea, now over a green isle. Swiftly they dropped down to the island and the eagle folded her wings and John climbed down.

"Now, John," she said, "be quick and fill your three bottles from that well while the black dogs that guard it are away."

John hurried to the well, and filled his three bottles with the clear gold water, and when he rose he saw a small house nearby. He thought he would go and see what was inside it, and in the first room he went into there was a bottle on a table. He filled a glass and the wine from the bottle was like sweet fire, and after he had drunk from it the bottle was still full.

"I will take that bottle with me, as well as the bottles of well water," he said, and he went on into the next room. Here there was a loaf of bread, and when he cut a slice the bread was like new corn, and the loaf was still whole.

"Dear Lord, I will not leave you," said John to the loaf, and he took it, with the bottles of well water and wine, and went into the third room. Here there was a great cheese, and when he broke a piece off it was like fairy cream, and the cheese was still whole, so he took it along with the water and the wine and the loaf. Behind the house he stepped out into a garden, and there amongst the flowers was the most beautiful woman he had ever seen.

"Ah, it would be a pain not to kiss you, my love," said John, and when he had kissed her they knew they loved each other, and they were married. For a week they lived in great happiness in the small house on the Green Isle, and then John knew he must go, though he promised that he would one day come back for his wife if it was possible. He climbed up between the eagle's wings and they flew back the way they had come, until they reached the house of the second giant. This giant was feasting all his friends and servants.

"Well, John," he said, "have you ever seen food and drink like this in the house of your father the king?"

"Hoo," said John. "I have drink here that is like it, but a thousand times better."

He gave the giant a drink from the bottle of wine, and the bottle was as full as ever.

"I will give you a hundred gold coins and a saddle and bridle for that bottle," said the giant.

"It is a bargain," said John, "but you must give it to my wife if she should come this way."

"I will do that," said the giant, so they said good-by, and the eagle carried John to the house of the first giant. He too was feasting his friends and servants, and asked John if he had ever seen food and drink like this before, and when John let him taste the bread and the cheese he was offered a hundred gold coins and a saddle and bridle for them.

"It is a bargain," said John, "but you must give them to my wife if she should come this way."

"I will do that," said the giant, so they said good-by, and the eagle carried John to the big town where he had left his brothers, and folded her wings and put him down. John thanked her for her help, and she thanked him for cutting off the wart from her ear, and before she had disappeared into the sky, there were his two brothers sauntering down the same street in which he had last seen them.

"Well, my brothers," said John, "since I have brought the water from the well at the edge of the world, we had better go home together. Here is a bridle and saddle for each of you, and here is money for a horse to fit them."

His brothers took the presents, but John did not give them the three bottles of water from the well on the Green Isle, and as they came near their home they decided to kill him. Without warning they attacked him, and beat him, and when they thought he was dead they threw him into a ditch by the side of the road and took the three bottles from him, and went on home.

John was not long in the ditch before his father's smith came along the road with a cartload of rusty iron.

John called out: "Oh, whatever Christian is passing, please give me some help." And the smith stopped his cart, and lifted John from the ditch, and threw him in amongst the rusty iron. He was covered with sores from his brothers' beating, and the rust went into the sores and took the skin off them, so that from his head to his feet he was rough-skinned, and even the hair of his head fell out. Nobody, not even his father, would have known him, and he went back to the smith's house, too ashamed to return to his own.

Meanwhile, on the Green Isle, the months passed and a son was born to the beautiful wife John had left behind; but she was sad, seeing this baby whose father had left so long before. So one day she took her baby to the wise woman who lived

near the well of gold water, and asked her, weeping, what she should do.

"Do not weep for the baby," said the hen-wife. "Here is a bird, and as soon as it sees the father of your child, it will hop on top of his head."

So John's wife took the bird, and her baby, and when someone had rowed her across the sea, she set out into the world to look for the father of her son. After some time she reached the house of the second giant, and asked for shelter, and when she went in she saw the bottle of wine on his table.

"Aiee, who gave you that bottle?" she asked.

"It was John, son of the king," said the giant.

"Then it is mine," she said, "for I am his wife."

As he had promised, the giant gave her the bottle, and she said good-by to him when she had rested for a day and a night, and with her baby and her bird she traveled on until she reached the house of the first giant. Again she asked for shelter, and when she went in she saw on his table the loaf and the cheese, and when she told the giant who she was he gave them to her. Now she need never go hungry or thirsty, and the journey seemed less long, and at last she reached the palace of the king.

"I have come from the Green Isle at the edge of the world," she told the king's servants, "to look for the father of my child." And they took her in and led her to the king. His eyes had recovered their sight, and his feet their strength, and when he heard of the beautiful woman's plight he ordered every man in his kingdom to be led through the palace. They poured through in hundreds, in at the front door and out by the back, but the bird never stirred from the woman's hand.

"Is there not a single other man in the country who is not here?" she asked.

"I have a bald, rough-skinned lad in my smithy," said the king's smith, "but. . . ."

"Rough or not, send him here," she said.

As soon as the bird saw the rough-skinned man come in she flew over and sat on his head, where the hair was only half-grown. The beautiful girl went over and held and kissed him.

"It is you who are the father of my child," she said.

"But John," said the king, "if you went to the Green Isle at the edge of the world, then it was you who fetched the water which brought back the sight of my eyes and the strength of my feet."

"Indeed it was I," said John.

"Then what shall I do with your two brothers who wronged you and lied to me?"

But by this time the two brothers had jumped on their horses and ridden away, and nobody saw them again. The king gave John and his wife a great, rich wedding, since they had not had one on the Green Isle, which lasted for seven days and seven nights. They invited the two giants, and the eagle, but the chief guest was the brown bear of the green glen, who came with the cinder in his mouth which he only took out to eat and to drink and to tell them stories. The small bird sang and the wine like sweet fire flowed from the bottle which never grew empty, and as far as I know it is flowing still.

BLACKBERRIES
IN FEBRUARY

There was a king before this, and when his first son was born, the queen died.

The king was stricken with grief, and he searched the kingdom and found fifteen children who were exactly like his son to be playmates for him, and fifteen nurses to watch over them.

After a while the king married again, and there was a new young queen in the palace. By this time the king's son and his fifteen companions were going to school, and one day when they were on their way home, driving balls before them with sticks, the young queen was on the road to meet them.

Also on the road was the Old Woman of the Hens, a wicked creature with magical powers.

"Oh ho," said the Old Hen Woman when she met the queen. "You are a luckless one, wife to the king. Though you may have many children of your own, none will be king, for there is the future king, driving a silver ball down the road with a stick of gold."

The queen looked at the young prince John and her face grew long. The Old Hen Woman came closer and whispered slyly:

"For a very small reward I will show you how to get rid of him."

"What reward would you want?" asked the queen.

"I should want to fill my little black bag with wool, and my little black crock with butter, and my little black shoe with meat."

112

"What would fill your little black bag with wool?" asked the queen.

"What comes from your shearing houses in seven years would fill it," said the Old Hen Woman.

"Oh, oh, it is large that little black bag of yours, but I will get the wool. And what would fill your little black crock with butter?"

"What comes from your cow houses in seven years would fill it," said the Old Hen Woman.

"Oh, oh, it is large that little black crock of yours, but I will get the butter. And what would fill your little black shoe with meat?"

"What comes from your slaughterhouses in seven years would fill it," said the Old Hen Woman.

"Oh, oh, it is large that little black shoe of yours, but large as it is I will get the meat," said the queen.

The Old Hen Woman came closer still.

"Put the prince under crosses and spells," she said, "and under the nine cow fetters of the world-wandering fairy woman,

> *so that water does not leave his shoe,*
> *nor will he rest his sight,*
> *and if he sleep one night*
> *he'll surely not sleep two,*
> *until he gets for you*
> THE WOOD THAT IS NEITHER CROOKED NOR STRAIGHT."

So when she got back to the palace the queen sent for John and she put him under crosses and spells, and under the nine cow fetters of the world-wandering fairy woman, to get for her the wood that was neither crooked nor straight.

113

Since it was a strong spell, John could do nothing but set off into the world, further than I am able to tell you, even if we talked till this time tomorrow. He walked, and he walked until

> *his soles were black as tar,*
> *his cheeks were thin and drawn,*
> *in walnut and in thorn*
> *each small brown bird was hiding,*
> *and on the night wind riding*
> *came dusky clouds from far,*
> *while clouds of day*
> *like wisps of hay*
> *blew off until the dawn.*

When he was nearly dead with tiredness, he saw a small light in the gloom, and went toward it. It came from a house, and when he knocked at the door he was surprised to be welcomed by the woman inside.

"Ah, son of the king," she said, "come in, come in. I am the sister of your mother. What has brought you from the town? Tell me."

He told her that he had been sent to find the wood that was neither crooked nor straight, and had searched the whole day and not found it.

The woman sat him down, and gave him food and drink, and washed his feet with water and milk, and dried them with a mantle of silk. She put him to bed at last with the Harp of Healing beside him to play him into deep soothing sleep that would take all his tiredness from him.

When the white morning came, she took him to a saw pit, and she filled a small bag with sawdust, and gave it to him and said:

114

"Give this to that luckless queen who put you under spells. It is wood that is neither crooked nor straight."

Prince John thanked her, and went back with a light heart and a springing step. The queen saw him coming down the road with the bag of sawdust, and she sent for the Old Hen Woman.

"He has broken the spell," she said. "He has got the wood that is neither crooked nor straight."

"Ah, do not despair," said the Old Hen Woman. "Put him under fresh crosses and spells, and under the nine cow-fetters of the world-wandering fairy woman,

> so that water does not leave his shoe,
> nor will he rest his sight,
> and if he sleep one night
> he'll surely not sleep two,
> until he gets for you
> BLACKBERRIES IN FEBRUARY."

So poor Prince John was put under fresh spells, and away he went again, and this time he went straight to the house of his mother's sister.

"Ah, poor John," said she, "I fear you will never return from this quest. Many kings and knights have gone to get these blackberries of special sweetness and power, but none returned to tell the story.

"There is only one place under the seven red stars of the world where these berries grow, and that is a room belonging to three giants. They grow there because of the heat of all the dead bodies the giants keep in that room."

When John heard where the blackberries could be found, he said he would have no rest nor peace till he got them, and sadly his mother's sister let him go. He walked and he walked until

his soles were black as tar,
his cheeks were thin and drawn,
in walnut and in thorn
each small brown bird was hiding,
and on the night wind riding
came dusky clouds from far,
while clouds of day
like wisps of hay
blew off until the dawn.

Then, when he was nearly dead with tiredness, he reached the giants' castle, and crept through a hole in one of the windows. At once he knew he was in the room where the blackberries grew, for it was full of bodies. Some were hanging up, some lying on the ground, the bodies of people the giants had killed and were going to eat.

Before he had time to start searching, there was the steerum, starum, stararick of the giants' footsteps as they returned home. The earth trembled, the doorposts shook, and in the walls of the castle the big stones danced against the little stones, and John just had time to throw himself down on the floor amongst the bodies when the giants arrived. And all round him on the ground were blackberries.

The giants sat down and ate some fish they had brought in, and very carefully John picked some of the blackberries and put them in his pocket. Then the biggest giant asked the smallest giant to cut a piece of meat from the fattest body he could find.

John lay very still, but the smallest giant came straight over to him and cut a slice from his leg, and took it to the biggest giant.

"Ah, ha," said the biggest giant, smacking his lips with the

116

sound of a waterfall. "This is the best flesh I ever ate. Put that body in the water butt and keep it fresh until we get back from our night's hunting. Then I will eat my fill."

Poor Prince John was picked up and dropped into a butt of water, and had to stay there till the giants went off again to hunt. Then he crept out, cold and aching, and made for the door.

He was halfway through it when he met one of the giants returning to fetch an arrow he had forgotten.

"Ho, ho, stranger," said the giant. "I have expected you for a long time. It was prophesied that you would come to steal our blackberries. Now I don't know what to do with you, for you are not worthy for me to eat."

The other giants came back to see what was happening, and they decided that the best thing to do with John was to tie him to a horse and let him be dragged along the ground, with dogs to chase and bite him as he went.

When this was done they picked up his battered body and threw it over the rocks, for they were sure he was dead.

But he was not dead, and what was there over the edge of the rocks but the nest of an eagle, and into this John fell. The nest was warm and every evening the eagle brought meat for her chicks, and John ate some of this, and his wounds healed.

When he was better he grew tired of the nest, and on a night of nights, and the eagle asleep, he tied himself to her claws with his belt. In the morning the eagle rose from her nest and flew off, with John tied under her, and the first place she alighted was the garden of John's father the king.

Prince John untied himself from the eagle, thanked her, and went into the palace, the blackberries in his pocket. The queen saw him and her face fell, and it fell even farther when he pulled out the gleaming blackberries. She hurried to the Old Hen

117

Woman and told her that the wanderer had returned, and with him the blackberries, though it was February.

"Oh, oh," said the Old Hen Woman, "someone wiser than himself is helping him. But do not despair, there is one spell left, the third. Put him under crosses and spells, and under the nine cow fetters of the world-wandering fairy woman,

> *so that water does not leave his shoe,*
> *nor will he rest his sight,*
> *and if he sleeps one night*
> *he'll surely not sleep two,*
> *until he gets for you*
> THE STEED OF CORRIE OF THE SHADOWS."

The queen called Prince John to her, and put him under crosses and spells, and under the nine cow fetters of the world-wandering fairy woman, to get the magic steed of the giant Corrie of the Shadows. But this time John felt strong, and he answered her:

"I put crosses and spells on you
That one of your feet will be in the palace
And the other foot in the kitchen.
One cheek full of barley,
The other full of salt water,
A goose feather in your nose
Blowing in every wind
Till I return."

And he left the queen like that, and off he went again to his mother's sister's house to find where Corrie of the Shadows lived. Again she told him with a heavy heart, and when he reached Corrie's castle he knocked at the door.

The giant himself answered, and John asked for work.

"Well, young lad, what is it you are good at?" asked the giant. John said he was a good stable boy, and the giant said this was what he needed, since the last boy had lost his head. He pointed to the head of the stable boy hanging on the wall, to show John what happened to people who tried to steal his magic steed.

For a few days John looked after the horse very carefully, and the giant was pleased with him. Then for a few days more he fed and groomed the beautiful horse. Then, on a night of nights and the giant asleep, he mounted and rode off.

Early next morning Corrie of the Shadows woke and went to the stable and saw it was empty. The steed was gone, and the stable boy was gone. Corrie put his whistle to his lips and blew it, and though John had ridden away fast, seven times faster the steed galloped him back.

"Ho, ho, son of the king," said the giant. "It was prophesied that you would come to steal my horse. Now I don't know whether to give you to the dogs, or to put you under the red-hot drippings of the great candles. I think I will put you under the candles."

He tied John up, and the first burning drop from the great candle fell on his right foot and cut it off.

"Have you ever been in such a bad way as this, John?" asked Corrie.

"Indeed I have," said John, "I went to search for the wood that was neither crooked nor straight, and I think that was harder for me than this."

"Oh no, it wasn't harder," said Corrie, and he let another burning drop fall from the great candle onto John's leg, cutting it off from the knee.

"Now, have you ever been in such a bad way as this, John?" he asked.

"Indeed I have," said John. "I went to look for blackberries in February, and some giants caught me, and threw me into a butt of water, and then they tied me to a horse and set dogs on me. After that they threw me over the rocks, and I was nine days and nine nights in the nest of an eagle. I was in a worse way than now, even though I am at your mercy."

Suddenly the giant's mother, who was sitting in the corner, spoke up.

"The king's son," she croaked. "It was his father who saved me from those same three giants who have the blackberries in February. Me and you, too, when you were a baby."

"A shroud on you, woman, why didn't you tell me this sooner?" said Corrie.

Then he got a bottle of healing medicine and made John as whole as ever he was, and gave him his steed, and a gilded saddle with it. He also gave him the Listening Chain, and at the first shake of it they heard the chimes in the five corners of Erin, as far as the Bridge of a Hundred Pardons.

Now, ever since Prince John had been put under spells and left the palace, his father the king had lain on a bed of darkness, with one-third of his strength gone, and one-third of his sight gone, and one-third of his hearing gone.

But when John shook the Listening Chain his father's sight returned, and when John's steed set his feet on the stones of his own city, his father's hearing returned, and when John came within sight of the palace his father's strength returned, and he leapt from his bed of darkness.

The queen was still standing with one cheek full of barley and another full of salt water, with a goose feather in her nose blowing in every wind. When she heard the hoofs of the steed of Corrie of the Shadows she trembled with fright, and so did the Old Hen Woman.

The king sent them both off into the woods to cut green oak for a fire to burn themselves, and as far as I know they are cutting it still.

THE MAN WHO
COULDN'T GET MARRIED

❧❦❧

There was before this a famous hunter called Murachag Mac Brian, who lived on the Plain of Pebbles. One day Murachag was out hunting when the mist came down, and he thought he would go into the woods to gather nuts until it lifted.

As he was searching for the nuts in the mist, he heard the stroke of an ax, and he went to see who it was, and it was a small man with a cap on his head.

He greeted the man.

"I am thinking," said the little man, "that you are of the tribe of Murachag Mac Brian."

"I am," said he.

"Then I will give you a share of the night's sleep even if you have the head of a man at your belt," said the little man, and because the mist was cold Murachag thanked him for the offer and they went back together to the woodman's house.

And what a house it was! The wife of the house brought up a chair of gold and put it under her husband, and she brought up a chair of silver and put it under Murachag. Then she brought a glass of wine and handed it to her guest, and when he had taken a drink she gave the glass to her husband who also drank from it, and then broke it against the wall. As they drank they talked together, and all the while Murachag could not help staring at the woodman's wife because she was a woman of great beauty.

"I am thinking," said the woodman at last, "that you are Murachag Mac Brian himself."

123

"I am," said he.

"I have done you two discourtesies since you came to the house, Murachag Mac Brian, and you have done one to me," said the woodman.

"What discourtesies are those?" said Murachag.

"I myself sat in the chair of gold and gave to you the chair of silver, and I shamed you by drinking from your glass before I broke it."

"And what was the discourtesy I did to you?"

"You have been gazing at my wife since you came into the house, and if you knew the trouble I had to get her, you would not wonder that I do not like another man to look at her."

"What is the trouble you had to get her?" asked Murachag, and at first the woodman said it was too long a tale to tell, but Murachag said not a cloud of sleep should cross his eyes till he had heard the story. So they settled in front of the fire and the woodman began his tale.

"For seven long years," he said, "I lived here in the woods on my own with no man but myself, nor woman either. On a day of days came a soothsayer down the road and said that I should set out to see the Old Woman of the island to find the answer to my loneliness, so on a summer's afternoon that is what I did. As I came near to the island the Old Woman was being attacked by a wild dog, and I ran and hit the dog with my heavy stick, and it left the Old Woman and ran off.

"The Island Gruagach was so grateful that she said she would give me her daughter in marriage, and a wedding was arranged that very night between myself and her beautiful daughter; but the fatigue of the fight and the evil of the drink overcame me, and I slept instead of marrying. It was early the day came, and early the girl's father woke me, shouting at me to go with him to his hunting hill. As we hunted on the hill I thought of the girl I had left at home with no one to guard her, and I left the hunting hill and hurried back. When I reached her home I found her mother the Island Gruagach crying, and I said to her: 'What is on you, oh woman?'

" 'Great trouble is on me,' she wailed. 'Three monks have just taken away the woman you were to marry.'

"Without waiting to hear more, I took the track of the duck to the shore, and there was my ship drawn up seven lengths on the shore where no wind could blacken her and no sun burn. I put my back to her and pushed her out, and gave her stern to the land and her prow to the sea, and at the first land I reached there were the three monks casting lots for my woman. I knocked their three heads together, and I took her and put her in the back of my boat.

"Then I raised the speckled sails against the mast, straight as an arrow, and my music was the cry of the gulls. The bent brown periwinkle cracked the keel of my ship as she sped through the water, and her prow could have cut a slender stalk of corn, and there was no stopping until we reached home.

"Another wedding was arranged that very night, and there was dancing, and drinking, and music that would bring relief to wounded men or make women in pain sleep like their babies. And the fatigue of the journey and the evil of the drink overcame me, and I slept instead of getting married. It was early the day came, and early the girl's father woke me, shouting at me to go with him to his hunting hill. As we hunted I thought of the girl I had left at home with no one to guard her, and I left the hill and hurried back.

"When I reached her home again I found her mother the Island Gruagach crying.

" 'What is on you this evening?' I asked.

" 'It is a great weight that is on me,' she wailed. 'The War-rior of the Wet Cloak has taken the woman you are to marry.'

"Without waiting to hear more I took the track of the duck again, and put my boat to sea, and did not stop until I reached the country of the Warrior of the Wet Cloak. I drew my boat seven lengths on the shore, where wind would not blacken nor sun burn, and I left my coat of mail and my spears under the side of the boat, and I started up the road to the town.

"As I walked a herdsman joined me.

" 'What is your news today, oh herdsman?' I said.

" 'Great and good news indeed, oh stranger,' said the herds-man. 'A wedding between the Warrior of the Wet Cloak and the daughter of the Island Gruagach. The first to the last in the land are invited.'

126

" 'If you will give me that patched cloak you wear, I will give you my good coat, and bless you withal,' I said to the herdsman. So the herdsman gave me his cloak, and I went up the hill to the palace where everyone was collected for the wedding, and nobody knew me for a stranger. I thought how lucky it was that they were all gathered together, for suddenly I swung my knife and tore through them, as a falcon through a flock, or as a goat up a rock, or as a dog through a drove of sheep on a cold spring day.

"I scattered them as clouds scattered by the wind, and reached my woman, and took her and carried her back to my boat. I raised the speckled sails against the mast, and my music was the cry of gulls and the plunge of eels. The bent brown periwinkle cracked the keel of my ship as she sped through the water, and she could have cut a slender stalk of corn with the swiftness of her passage.

"When we reached home another wedding was arranged that very night, and there was dancing and drinking and music to lay all sorrow at rest. But the fatigue of the fight and the evil of the drink overcame me, and I slept instead of getting married. It was early the day came, and early the girl's father woke me, shouting at me to go with him to his hunting hill. As we hunted I thought of the girl I had left at home with no one to guard her, and I hurried home, and I found her mother crying.

" 'What is on you again?' I asked.

" 'It is the greatest weight of all that is on me,' she wailed. 'The Son of the King of Light has taken the woman you are to marry.'

"Without waiting to hear more, I took the track of the duck, and put my ship to sea, and did not stop until I reached the country of the King of Light. I drew my boat seven lengths on

128

the shore, where wind could not blacken nor sun burn, and I left my coat of mail and my shield and my spears under the side of the boat, and started up the road to the palace.

"As I walked, a beggar joined me.

" 'What is your news today, oh beggar?' I said.

" 'It is great and good news I have,' said the beggar. 'A great wedding between the Son of the King of Light and the daughter of the Island Gruagach, and the first to the last in the kingdom are invited.'

" 'If you would give me your coat, I would pay you well and give you this good coat of mine in exchange,' I said to the beggar. So we exchanged coats and I went up to join all the other beggars who were gathered to be fed at the wedding.

"I sat myself amongst the beggars, and when the food was thrown I caught each piece, and with my free hand I caught all the drink. The beggars complained, but in the end they were all satisfied and went away, but I lay down on the ground in front of the palace.

" 'The big beggar who took all the food and all the drink is lying drunk on the ground,' they told the bridegroom, and he told his servants to lift me and throw me into a ditch. Five men came to lift me, but by your own two hands, oh Murachag, it would have been easier to lift Candle Cairn from the ground than me. In the end the Son of the King of Light came down, and he lifted my cap, and he saw the mole on my forehead. No one who had seen that mole would forget it, and he knew who I was.

" 'Fortune help me tonight,' he said. 'This is Straight Sinewed of the Glen, a man without mercy and without fear of God or of man.'

"Then I rose and went to my boat, and put on my charmed shirt of smooth yellow silk, and my chain coat above it, my bright blue coat, dart-resisting, flawless. I put on my helmet to hide the mole on my forehead, and took my pointed shield in my left hand, and in my right hand my hero's sword, and at my belt my cluster of narrow knives.

"I went up to meet the Son of the King of Light, and we fought until the mouth of the night, when half the color had drained from the sky, and though he tried to stab the mole in my forehead he could not pierce my helmet. I thought how far I was from my friends, and only my enemies around me in a strange country, and at last my sword pierced his shoulder. The Son of the King of Light fell at my feet, but I did not stop to lift him.

"I took my woman and carried her back to my boat, and raised the speckled sails against the tall mast. My music was the cry of gulls and the wind in the ropes; the bent brown periwinkle cracked the keel of my ship as she sped through the water, and she could have cut a slender stalk of corn with the swiftness of her passage.

"We did not stop until we reached home, and then at last I married the daughter of the Island Gruagach, and was at rest. We returned here to live, and she brought much gold and silver with her. Is it a wonder, oh Murachag, that I do not care to have another man stare at her?"

"Indeed it is no wonder," said Murachag, and he went to his bed pondering how the little man in the brown cap could be Straight Sinewed of the Glen, a man without mercy and without fear of God or of man. But in the morning when the mist had lifted he said good-by to his host, and the woodman lifted his cap and he saw the mole on his forehead. Then, although he was a famous hunter, Murachag Mac Brian shivered, and he made up his mind that never again would he stare at the wife of a woodman, however small. As far as I know he never has.

THE KNIGHT
OF THE RED SHIELD

There was a king before this, and on a day of days he and his warriors and his nobles and his gentlemen went to his hunting hill. They sat themselves on a green hillock, where the sun rose early and sank late, and while they rested there one of the king's nobles said:

"Who now, in the four brown quarters of the world, would have the heart to disgrace our king amongst his people?"

"You are foolish, and you speak rashly," said the king. "Such a man would come, and would disgrace me, and would be gone before one of you was able to pluck a hair from his beard."

Even as the king spoke, the shadow of a shower came out of the west and traveled eastward, and behind it a great black horse with a huge man mounted on it.

> As a warrior on a mountain shore,
> As a great star over little stars,
> As a wide sea over small pools,
> As the coal of a smith's fire
> Quenched at the bank of a river,
> In figure, in form, in face
> Was he greater than all the men of the world.

The rider approached, and spoke to the king in the quiet words of true wisdom, in the gentle words of deep knowledge, and then before the king could answer, he struck him between the mouth and the nose. The blow drove out three teeth, and he caught them in his fist, and put them in his bag, and rode away.

For a moment they were all too stunned to speak, then the king found his voice.

"Did I not say that a man would come, and would disgrace me, and would be gone before one of you was able to pluck a hair from his beard?" he said.

The king's eldest son, the Knight of the Cairn, stepped forward, and kneeling at his father's feet he swore that he would not eat meat, nor taste drink, nor hear music, until he had taken from the shoulders the head of the man who had planned this deed.

Then the king's second son knelt and swore that he too would starve. "I," said the Knight of the Sword, "will take the hand from the shoulder of the man who struck the king."

Then a third man stepped out, who was neither a prince nor a noble, but only a serving man, and who was known as the Son of the Spring. He also knelt at the king's feet, and swore that he would wrench out the heart of the man who had planned the insult to his king.

"Who are you, impudent creature, to think you can join us in our quest?" said the Knight of the Cairn. "When we were brave you would be weak. You would meet your death in a peat bog, or in the rift of a rock, or at the bottom of a cliff."

"Be that as it may, I shall go with you," said the Son of the Spring.

The king's sons laughed at his impudence, and went to prepare themselves for their journey. When they had collected their weapons they said farewell to their father and set off, but they had not gone far when the Knight of the Cairn glanced round and saw the Son of the Spring following.

"What," said the Knight of the Cairn, "shall we do with him?"

"Do?" said the Knight of the Sword. "Sweep his head off."

"No, we won't do that. There is a great rock down there; we will tie him to it."

So they tied the Son of the Spring to the rock and left him to die, and went on their way, but they had not gone far when the Knight of the Cairn glanced round and saw him following, with the rock on his back.

"What," said the Knight of the Cairn, "shall we do with him now?"

"Sweep his head off," said the Knight of the Sword.

"We won't do that. We need a servant to polish a shield and blow up a fire. We'll untie the rock from his back; it will be an easy matter for two great heroes like us. Then we'll let him come with us as our servant."

So they untied the rock, and took the Son of the Spring with them, and continued on their way until they reached the seashore. Here was tied their boat, a painted ship of the yew tree, and they drew up her anchor and the three of them got aboard.

They put her prow to the wave, her stern to the sand,
Hoisted red banners, made her speckled sails billow,

And rode to a breeze that would draw the roots from
*   the willow*
A wind to bring heather from the barren land.

And lure from trees their leaves
And ruffle thatch about the cottage eaves.

So that the green silk waves were split and torn,
As a knife cuts the corn

The crooked whelks against her planks colliding
When like an arrow from a bow of magic yew,
*   forward and onward she went riding.*

For three days they sailed like this, then:

"I am growing tired of this," said the Knight of the Cairn. "It is time to get news from the mast."

"You are the eldest and the bravest, oh Knight of the Cairn," said the Son of the Spring. "You may have the honor of going up."

So up the mast with a rush went the Knight of the Cairn, and down he came with a clatter onto the deck of the ship.

"That was very badly done," laughed his brother the Knight of the Sword.

"Let us see if you can do better then," said the elder prince, picking himself up.

So up the mast went the Knight of the Sword, and he had only gone halfway when he began squealing and yelling that he could not go up or come down.

"I am no warrior, nor even half a warrior," said the Son of the Spring. "You said I would find death in a peat bog or in the rift of a rock or at the foot of a cliff. But it would be no trouble to me to get news from the mast."

"Oh great hero," sneered the princes. "Try it."

So the Son of the Spring measured a spring from the end of his spear to the points of his toes, and he was up on the crossbeams in a twinkling.

"What do you see?" asked the Knight of the Cairn.

"It is too big for a crow and too little for land," said he.

"Stay where you are and try to find out what it is."

So the Son of the Spring stayed at the top of the mast for a while.

"What are you seeing now?" said the Knight of the Cairn.

"It is an island with a circle of fire round it, flaming at either end. And I am thinking there is not a warrior in the great world could go across that fire."

"Two heroes such as we could easily manage it," said the princes, and they steered the painted ship to the windward side of the fire, and drew her up seven lengths on gray grass. Then they made a round fire and gave three days and three nights to their tiredness.

At the end of three days, they began to sharpen their arms.

"I," said the Knight of the Cairn, "am beginning to grow tired of this. It is time to get news of the island."

"You are the eldest and the bravest, oh Knight of the Cairn," said the Son of the Spring. "Go first and see what news you can bring of the island."

So the Knight of the Cairn approached the fire, and tried to leap over it, and went down in it up to his knees. When he came out there was not a hair between his knees and his ankles, and his skin was in crumpled folds around his shoes.

"That was very badly done," laughed the Knight of the Sword.

"Let us see if you can do better then," said the elder prince, rubbing his smarting legs.

So the Knight of the Sword approached the fire and tried to leap over it, and went in it up to his thighs. When he came out there was not a hair between his thighs and his ankles, and his skin was in crumpled folds around his shoes.

"Well," said the Son of the Spring, "I am no warrior nor even half a warrior, but if I had my choice of arms, it would be no hardship to me to get news of the island."

"You may take our arms," said the princes, and they clothed

135

him in a gold silk shirt, and above it a coat of chain. They gave him a pointed shield of red copper, and a helmet, and a champion's strong sword, and a surety knife sharp against his waist.

He ran up the shore, his feet lifting turfs behind him like a plow in the earth, and he measured a spring from the end of his spear to the points of his toes, and he leapt clean across the fire. And he was on the island he had dreamed of, the one island of the world.

He crossed the island and saw a small hill, golden in the sun, and on the hill a woman like a jewel sitting with the head of a sleeping man in her lap. He went up and spoke to her gently and politely, and she answered him in the same way, and when they had talked for a while she said:

"I have been waiting for a man like you. If I had my choice you would not leave the island."

"Then you will tell me what is waking for that young man?" said the Son of the Spring.

"It is to take off the end of his little finger," said the jewel of a woman.

The Son of the Spring took his surety knife from his belt, and he cut off the man's finger from the root, but he did not shrink or stir.

"Tell me truly what is waking for the young man, or you and he will lose your heads," said the Son of the Spring.

"Waking for him," she said, "is something you cannot do, nor any other warrior except the Knight of the Red Shield. There is a prophesy that he will come to the island, a man without baptism, and will lift that great stone over there and drop it onto this man's chest."

As she spoke, strength and power struck the Son of the Spring like a fist, for he had a red shield, and was unbaptized.

He went to the great stone, and lifted it in his two hands, and dropped it on the chest of the sleeping man. The man opened his eyes and gave him a slow stare.

"Ah," he said. "You have come, Knight of the Red Shield, for from today that is your name. You will not long stand up to me in a fight."

He rose, and they began to wrestle, and fought together till the mouth of the night, when half the color had drained from the sky and they were nearly dead with tiredness. Then the Knight of the Red Shield thought of night coming on, and how he was far from his friends, alone on this strange island with an enemy, and he gave a last heave and flung him to the ground. Then with three sweeps he took the man's hand from his shoulder, the heart from his chest, and the head from his neck, for he thought this was the man who had insulted his king.

He put his hand into the bag the man carried, and found three old horse's teeth, and thought these were the king's teeth, and took them with him. Then he went to a wood nearby and broke off a branch from a tree and tied to it the head and the hand and the heart.

"Which would you rather do?" he asked the jewel of a woman. "Stay on this island, or come with me?"

"I would rather go with you than with any man in the world," she said, so he raised her onto his shoulders, which were like mountaintops where showers fall, and carried her back across the fire.

The Knight of the Cairn and the Knight of the Sword saw him coming, and they were angry that he had done what they could not do.

"A great warrior must have been chasing you, and turned

137

back when he saw two heroes like us waiting for him," they sneered.

"Here," said the Knight of the Red Shield. "A jewel of a woman, and the three teeth of your father, and the hand and the heart and the head of the man whose fist struck them from him. Wait for me here awhile, for I want to see the whole island before we go."

He leapt again through the fire, and started across the island, but when he looked back he saw the painted ship playing hide-and-seek with the waves as it sailed away.

"Death's wrappings on you," he swore. "A tempest of blood in your eyes, the ghost of your hanging on you, for leaving me on an island by myself without knowing where I shall go for the night."

He walked and he walked, and though it was nearly dark he did not see a single house nor tower where he could get shelter. Then at last, in a dark glen, he came across an old castle, and as he went forward to explore it he saw three young men coming wearily toward it, dragging their feet heavily as they trudged along. He spoke to them in quiet, gentle words, and they replied in the same way, and they sat together for a while, talking about themselves. While they talked of old times, it turned out that these were his own three foster brothers who had sailed away the year before and never returned. When they discovered this they were filled with joy, and the Knight of the Red Shield returned with them to their castle, and ate and drank and listened to music most of the night.

In the morning he woke and took food, and while he was eating he heard the clash of arms, as of men preparing to go to battle. It was his foster brothers and he asked them where they were going.

"Alas," said they. "We have been a year and a day on this island, waging war against the Son of Darkness and the Son of Dimness. Their mother is a witch, and has put us under a spell not to leave the island till we have killed them and their men, but if we kill all of them today, they will be alive tomorrow, for she has the power to bring them to life."

"I will go with you today," said the Knight of the Red Shield. "I will be able to help you."

"Then you will have to go alone," they said. "For it is part of the spell that whoever helps us must do it alone."

"Then I will go alone," said he. "You stay here today."

The Knight of the Red Shield went off alone to meet the Sons of Dimness and Darkness, and one after the other he killed their men, and in the end he met the two sons of the witch themselves.

"Is it you, oh Knight of the Red Shield?" said the Son of Darkness.

"It is I," he said.

"Well then, let us to battle. You will not stand up long against me."

They began to wrestle, and fought until the mouth of the night, when half the color had drained from the sky and they were nearly dead with tiredness; and then with a last mighty heave the Knight of the Red Shield lifted the Son of Darkness threw him to the ground and swept off his head. Then quickly he turned and swept off the head of the Son of Dimness, too, and their thirteen sons, each of them warrior of a hundred battles.

But though his enemies were dead, the Knight of the Red Shield was himself wounded and bleeding, and lay all that night and the next day amongst the fallen, too weak to move. The

battlefield was above the seashore, and as he lay there the sea beneath began to glow like a fiery brand, and hiss like a serpent, and roar like a bellowing bull. And from the sea rose the strangest, fiercest old woman he had ever seen.

She had one tooth longer than the great staff in her hand, and another shorter than the pin in her skirt, and he knew at once that this must be the witch who had put his foster brothers under a spell. She went straight to her two sons, of Darkness and Dimness, and placed a finger in their mouths and those of most of their men, and they rose up as alive as they had ever been. Then she came over to him and put her finger in his mouth, and he bit it off from the joint.

This made her very angry, and she put the point of her shoe under him and lifted him over seven ridges.

"Oh impudent one," she said. "You are the only one who will die on this battlefield."

The Knight of the Red Shield felt helpless as he lay where she had kicked him, and she strode toward him to finish him off. Then he thought of the sharp spear which he had stolen from her son, and he threw it with all his strength at her, and took off her head. And at the sight of her headless body, her sons and all their men fled in terror.

But the Knight of the Red Shield was still lying wounded on the battlefield, his blood spilt, his sinews torn, only his white bones whole.

And as he lay there, what did he see but a harper approaching him.

"What do you want?" he asked the harper.

"I am sure you are tired," said the harper. "Come down and lay your head on this little hillock, and I will play you to sleep and healing."

He crawled down, and lay with his head in the harper's lap, and closed his eyes and snored, as if he slept, but he was wide awake to his toes.

"You are dreaming," said the harper.

"I am," he murmured.

"What do you see in your dream?"

"I see a harper drawing a rusty old sword to take off my head," said he, and he leapt up and grabbed the harp and drove it against the harper's head, knocking his brains out. Then once more he fell exhausted on the battlefield.

Soon he heard the sound of weeping.

"Who is that?" said he.

"It is we, your foster brothers, who have been searching all day for you."

"I am lying here," he said, "my blood and flesh and sinews destroyed."

They came over to him and wept even louder when they saw his wounds.

"Ah, if only we had the vessel of healing balsam that belongs to the old witch, the mother of the Sons of Darkness and Dimness, we would heal you in a moment," they said.

"Look up there," said the Knight of the Red Shield, "that is her, lying dead. Anything she has is yours."

"We are free of our spells forever," cried the foster brothers joyfully, and they went to where the witch was lying, and took from her pocket the vessel of healing balsam she always carried.

Then they washed the Knight of the Red Shield with the balsam, and he rose as strong as he had ever been, and they all went back to the castle together, and spent the night in great rejoicing. In the morning they went out to play a game of shinty, but as they played, the shadow of a shower came out of the

west and traveled to the east, and behind it a great black horse
with a man mounted on it.

> As a warrior on a mountain shore,
> As a great star over little stars,
> As a wide sea over small pools,
> As the coal of a smith's fire
> Quenched at the bank of a river,
> In figure, in form, in face
> Was he greater than all the men of the world.

The great rider rode down to where they were standing.

"It was I," he said, "who took the three teeth from your
king, but you would be foolish, Knight of the Red Shield, to
wrestle with me for them."

"Why is that?" said the Knight.

"No man in the world will kill me unless he strikes me
straight through the heart," said he, and he was so tall that no
man could ever reach to strike him so high.

The Knight of the Red Shield took his sword, and he struck
at the earth, two blows, two stabs, two thrusts, and then he
stepped back. At the same moment his enemy stepped forward,
straight into the hole he had made in the ground, and with one
sweep he lopped off the rider's head. He put his hand into his
pouch, and he found the king's three teeth, and he took them
and went back to the castle.

"Find me some way of leaving the island," he said to his
foster brothers. "I have the teeth and I must return."

They begged him to stay, but he would not, so they gave
him a boat which could be turned round and would sail back
on its own, and three pigeons for company across the sea. They

bade him good-by sadly, but said they would soon be following him. When he reached land he turned the boat round and freed the pigeons and looked for the last time on the island with the circle of fire around it.

He set off straightaway for the king's palace and as he approached, cries of pain reached him on the road. When he entered, the Knight of the Cairn and the Knight of the Sword were seated on each side of the king, and the jewel of a woman in front. The two princes looked black as thunder when they saw him, but he took no notice of them and went straight to kneel before the king.

"What, oh king," he said, "are the shouts and cries of pain I have heard since I arrived, and even before, as I was approaching the palace?"

"Alas," said the king, "for more than a week my sons have been trying to drive three horse's teeth into my head with a hammer. My head has nearly split in two with the torment."

"What would you give to the man who could put your own teeth into your head without hurt?" said he.

"Half my kingdom while I live, and the whole when I am dead," said the king.

So the Knight of the Red Shield asked for a glass of water, and he put the teeth into the water, and he told the king to drink a draft. The king drank, and his teeth went back into his head, strongly and firmly, each tooth into its right place.

"Ah," sighed the king. "I am at rest at last. You are the one who did the brave deeds, not my pair of sons."

"Indeed it was he," said the jewel of a woman. "Not your shambling sons who stretched themselves out on the shore like seaweed-seekers while he fought their battles."

"I will not eat meat nor drink draft," said the king, "until men have collected faggots of gray oak to burn my sons."

145

But in the morning, who was first on his knees by the king's bed but the Knight of the Red Shield.

"Rise from your knees, knight," said the king. "Whatever one thing it is you want, you will get it."

"The one thing is the freeing of your sons," said he.

So the king let the princes go, and the Knight of the Red Shield married the jewel of a woman, and a great wedding was made for a year and a day. His foster brothers came from the island to join the celebrations, and the last day of it was as good as the first day.

IRIS MACFARLANE was born in Quetta (in what is now Pakistan) and lived in India for many years. Today she makes her home on the Isle of Uist in the Outer Hebrides. It was here, in entirely appropriate surroundings, that she set about the enormous task of making available to children the findings of the celebrated folklorist J. F. Campbell.

Mrs. Macfarlane is the author of *Tales and Legends of India*, *The Children of Bird God Hill* and *The Summer of the Lame Seagull*.

JOHN LAWRENCE attended Hastings School of Art and the Central School of Art in England, and then established himself as a free-lance illustrator and wood-engraver. His first picture book, *The Giant of Grabbist*, appeared in 1968. He has since then created three more picture books of his own and illustrated many other distinguished children's books. Among them are the established classics published by the London Folio Society and the Imprint Society of Massachusetts. In 1972, he was a second-prize winner in the Francis Williams Book Illustration Award.